THE GARUD STRIKES

An alumnus of La Martiniere College, Lucknow, the National Defence Academy, Pune, and the Indian Military Academy, Dehradun, Mukul Deva was commissioned in December 1981, into the Sikh Light Infantry of the Indian Army. He took early retirement from the Army after fifteen years of service, including a decade of combat operations in India and overseas. Now settled in Singapore and widely acknowledged as the 'Change Maker', Deva is an entrepreneur, motivational speaker and an executive, business and creativity coach. He has also served as a mentor with the United Nations Institute for Training and Research (UNITAR), Afghanistan Fellowship.

Other books written by Mukul Deva:

Time After Time … It All Happened, (Minerva, 2000)
M.O.D.E.L.: The Return of the Employee, (Sage, 2006)
Lashkar, (HarperCollins India, 2008)
Salim Must Die, (HarperCollins India, 2009)
Blowback, (HarperCollins India, 2010)
Tanzeem, (HarperCollins India, 2011)
The Dust Will Never Settle (HarperCollins India, 2012)
S.T.R.I.P.T.E.A.S.E: The Art of Corporate Warfare, (Marshall Cavendish, 2012)
R.I.P. (Westland Ltd, 2012)
F.C.U.K. Your Way To Success (Westland Ltd & Marshall Cavendish, 2013)
Weapon Of Vengeance (Macmillan, USA, 2014)
And Death Came Calling (HarperCollins India, 2014)

For more about the author, please visit his website www.mukuldeva.com

'The God of all things… it is tough describing Mukul Deva.'

- Business World

'Deva has a Nostradamus touch.'

- The Statesman

'India's literary storm trooper.'

- Business Standard

'You can smell the gunpowder. Such is the power of the words of Mukul Deva… India's first military action thriller writer.'

- The Hindu

'Here comes India's Clancy or Ludlum or Forsyth.'

- Outlook

'Mukul Deva wears the crown of India's premier military thriller writer with great skill and panache.'

- www.indepepal.com

'India finally has a writer of international caliber in the genre of military fiction.'

- First City

'Deva is a quintessential literary storm trooper… his books are fast-paced thrillers that have broken new ground.'

-Yuva

MUKUL DEVA

The Garud Strikes

First published by westland ltd in 2014

Published by Westland Books, a division of Nasadiya Technologies Private Limited, in 2024

No. 269/2B, First Floor, 'Irai Arul', Vimalraj Street, Nethaji Nagar, Alapakkam Main Road, Maduravoyal, Chennai 600095

Westland and the Westland logo are the trademarks of Nasadiya Technologies Private Limited, or its affiliates.

ISBN: 9789360451844

10 9 8 7 6 5 4 3 2 1

The views and opinions expressed in this work are the author's own and the facts are as reported by him, and the publisher is in no way liable for the same.

Typeset by PrePSol Enterprises Pvt. Ltd

Printed at Saurabh Printers Pvt. Ltd

DEDICATION

This book is a testimonial of Mrs Jane Himmeth Singh's dedication to her late husband, Lieutnant General Himmeth Singh PVSM.

And to the valiant officers and men of 4 Guards (1 Rajput).

To acknowledge the debt of honour that India owes to these brave men and their families, the proceeds of this book will be used for the welfare of these veterans, war widows and their children

CONTENTS

FOREWORD

Major Mukul Deva has written this book in the style of a raconteur talking in a fireside manner. Mrs.Jane Himmeth Singh, the widow of Lt.Gen. Himmeth Singh has been of great help to the author providing resources and encouragement for writing this book. The author discussed the operations of 4 GUARDS erstwhile I RAJPUT in the Bangladesh war of 1971, four decades earlier with its surviving officers who had taken part in that war. They recalled their own experience in that war and acts of gallantry and supreme sacrifice made by their comrades in that lightening war. They also recalled various personal and humorous incidents which showed the bonhomie and team spirit among the officers of the battalion. This must have been forged and promoted by their then Commanding Officer, Lt.Col. Himmeth Singh. Such camaraderie among Officers in a unit can be a battle winning factor. The author got a lot of material from a CD among the papers of late Colonel Pyara Lal recording the interview he had with Himmeth Singh soon after that war. With all this material he has put together a day by day account of the battalion's operations starting from Agartala across a most difficult riverine terrain and reaching the outskirts of Dhaka. The battalion led the advance of 4 Corps which culminated in the improvised heliborne operation across the formidable Meghna River to Dhaka. This hastened the surrender of 92,000 Pakistani soldiers at Dhaka and the birth of a new Nation. The gripping account of these operations brings to life the horrors of war and how surmounting all odds, the Indian Army won a most decisive victory in the country's history of thousands of years. Despite being flush with modern weapons holding various well prepared strong points on the border, the Pakistan Army was trounced and lost the will to fight.

The day by day account graphically brings out the gripping record of the battalion in that war. Starting with millions of refugees pouring into India with horrible stories of atrocities and genocide. 4 GUARDS was involved in that war from Day One when 4 GUARDS took part in the battle against Pakistan's heavily defended position at Akhaura to the end of that war. This book provides a good and detailed insight to the India's major thrust from Agartala to Dhaka. Throughout these operations Himmeth Singh led his battalion from the front, proving to be an excellent battlefield commander. I had the privilege of knowing Himmeth for many years serving at different places. He was a few years junior to me. I remember him when he was a young officer doing the Junior Commander's tactical course at the Infantry School Mhow now called War College. Later he did the staff course at Defence Services Staff College at Wellington. I was an instructor at both these institutions and he was with me in my syndicate. He was the best student at these courses befitting his earlier record of having won the Sword of Honour at the Indian Military Academy. He combined professional excellence with all the qualities of an officer and a gentleman. In 1982, Himmeth was the Corps Commander at Bhatinda when I was the Western Army Commander. I can vouch for the contribution made by him in the training and preparation for war of his Corps under his leadership. I took premature retirement from the Army in 1983. A few years later Himmeth was appointed Commandant of the prestigious National Defence College. I had just returned from being Ambassador in Kathmandu and Himmeth invited me to address the college on Indo Nepal relations. I found him very popular and much respected by students of that College.

That was my last interaction with him. After reading this book my esteem for him has gone higher for his achievement in command of 4 GUARD in battle. His battalion was rightly chosen to provide a guard of honour for the then Eastern Army Commander, Lt.Gen. Jagjit Singh Aurora, on his arrival at Dhaka for taking the surrender of Pakistani Commander in East Pakistan (Bangladesh). It was also in the fitness of things that he should be commanding the Parade at Dhaka at which the President of newly liberated Bangladesh, Sheikh Mujibur Rehman took the salute. These recognitions and the gallantry awards given to the personnel of the Battalion were in the fitness of things. However I feel that giving its Commanding Officer, Lt.Col. Himmeth Singh only a Mention in Dispatches was an inadequate recognition of his outstanding record in that war.

This book also highlights the plight of the war widows of the Battalion. The nation owes a debt to these widows who suffered the trauma of losing their husbands who sacrificed their lives for the Nation. During this war I was the Deputy Adjutant General at Army Headquarters on the staff of the then Army Chief, General S. H. F. J. Manekshaw dealing with man power planning for war and other personnel matters including pension for war widows. We worked out a generous scheme for war widows and war orphans of the Army. Apart from lump sum grants the widows became entitled to the full pay of their martyred husband till the latter's deemed date of retirement and full pension for the rest of their lives. A special provision was also made that the children of the soldiers killed in the war will be entitled to free education at any school including free boarding, school uniform and textbooks. When I briefed the three Chiefs of Staff regarding the new pension code, Gen.Manekshaw cracked a joke saying that at this rate Army wives will be happy to have their husbands dead rather than alive. Besides pension, State Governments chipped in to provide other concessions like petrol pumps and gas agencies for widows and also monetary grants. I am mentioning this because there is a reference in this book to some widows of the battalion in a difficult pecuniary condition.

This book is a captivating record of success by a battalion under good leadership in war. It is inspirational for young Army Officers and it affords a good glimpse of the achievements of a successful battalion in war.

New Delhi, Lt. Gen. (Retd) S.K.Sinha, PVSM
15th June 2014 (Former Governor of Assam and J & K)

ACKNOWLEDGEMENTS

It would have been impossible to complete this book without the unstinted help and support of Mrs Jane Himmeth Singh, who not only provided the resources and material but also constant encouragement. The manner in which she so diligently gathered and safeguarded all the materials and photographs used here amply highlight that this book is a labour of love, and her way of acknowledging her husband.

My special thanks also to the following:

Major Chandrakant, whose amazing, almost photographic, memory was able to provide minute details of the battalion's action. His insights as the then acting second-in-command were especially invaluable. He was remarkably diligent in locating and recording interviews of veterans and widows of the martyrs. In several places he even carried out interviews on my behalf, and so I ended up seeing the war and the people through his eyes.

Ms Bhawna Adhikari, wife of Colonel Rajesh Adhikari, of 4 Guards, who was not only a great source of encouragement but also an active participant in this project. She even made the trip to Bangladesh with Mrs Himmeth and Major Chandrakant and travelled the route that the battalion had taken during the war of liberation.

The veterans of 4 Guards (1 Rajput) who helped me restructure the confusing mass of information in the two years that it took to put this book together. I would like to especially commend the war widows, who took out the time and made the effort to travel long distances at such short notices to provide forgotten details that enrich this book.

Though I never had the pleasure of meeting him, Late Colonel Pyarelal, the Secretary of USI (United Service Institution of India), Delhi, also deserves a special mention. The recordings he had made of his conversations with General Himmeth Singh provided invaluable insights into the thoughts, considerations and fears that occupied Himmeth's mind during those tumultuous days when he led his men through the 1971 Indo-Pak war. They helped to generate a more complete and clearer picture of this enigmatic man. This wealth of information was very nearly lost. In fact, it only saw the light of day when the ever-perseverant Major Chandrakant went looking for them after the demise of Colonel Pyarelal. He found them in an old, abandoned briefcase. These recordings, which Himmeth's son, Mrityunja, later painstakingly transcribed, provided not just a detailed account of the strike of the Garud across Bangladesh, but also a bird's eye view of Himmeth's own thoughts and feelings.

Lieutenant General Shamsher Mehta (Retd.) for the war photos that he had, and those he obtained from the ever-obliging Mr Jayant Ulal, war correspondent of Stern magazine, Germany. Meeting the General, who, despite the passage of years, has lost none of the elan and josh that makes an Indian Army officer stand apart, was inspiring, to say the least.

Major Rajendra Mohan for introducing us to his Bangladeshi friends, like Mr Amin Bhai, who not only organized our trip to Bangladesh, but also provided constant support.

Major General J.P. Singh of the 31 Armoured Division, Brigadiers Bhanot and P. K. Singh of the Rajput Regimental Centre, and Honorary Captain Patiram Pal of 4 Guards for helping us gather the war veterans and widows, and interviewing them.

Major General Ravi Nair, Military Attache at the Indian High Commission in Dacca, who organized an evening at his home for us to meet the Bangladeshi citizens who had been victimised during the war.

Last, but not the least, to Gautam Padmanabhan, Vipin Vijay, Karthik Venkatesh, Shatrughan Pandey and Rahul Tanwar at Westland India for making this book possible.

AUTHOR'S NOTE

This book is not the story of the 1971 Indo-Pak War — of who won or who lost. It is the story of a few good men. The men of the 4th battalion of The Brigade of Guards, which was originally raised as the 2/15 BNI (Bengal Native Infantry) on 15 September 1798 at Sasaram, Bihar, and then re-designated on 26 January 1950 by General K.M. Cariappa, the then Commander-in-Chief of the Indian Army, as 4 Guards (1 Rajput).

These were not extraordinary men; they were simple, ordinary men like you and me. Men who laugh when happy, cry when sad, and bleed when hurt. But, like soldiers the world over, more often than not, their cries go unheard. These were and are men with families, which wait for them when they leave home for distant frontiers. And very often, wait in vain.

These were men who, when caught up in extraordinary circumstances, displayed exemplary courage and unfaltering devotion to duty. When the push came to a shove, they unfailingly rose to the occasion, with complete disregard for life and limb. That is what made them extraordinary, and inspired me to tell this tale.

It is hard for someone who has not been in battle, who has not seen blood and mangled bones, who has not been assaulted by the stench of death, who has not had a comrade die in their arms, to understand what wars can do to a man. Hence this book — to let you know what these brave men endure … for you … so that the nation stays secure.

While narrating this story, I have at all times maintained factual accuracy, and have not taken any artistic liberties.

However, since I was not present at the actual scene, and four decades have gone by, at times reality may have been clouded in the fog of battle, and in the fading memories of those who narrated these stories to me.

The Garud Strikes is my humble tribute to the forgotten brave hearts of 4 Guards (1 Rajput). To dwell on the lives of those who were martyred and those (parents, widows and orphans) they left behind; whose pain and loss is often not recognized. I would like them to know that they are alive in our hearts, that their sacrifice matters, and that the nation cares. And to remind India that it needs to care.

This book is also my humble tribute to the Indian Army, the organization that nurtured me and reinforced the values that my mother had bred in me. That gave me the discipline, focus and adaptability one needs to succeed. That taught me to keep going, no matter how adverse the situation, or how grim the odds. That conditioned me to make success a habit.

I must also stress that neither have any classified or official records been used in the writing of this book, nor have any serving officers, JCOs (Junior Commissioned Officers) or ORs (Other Ranks) been interviewed. I have relied solely on material available in the public domain (the Internet, books, newspaper and magazine articles), and the interviews of the veterans who took part in this campaign, their widows and orphans.

I have tried to use only those stories that have been verified by at least two independent sources, and have used the best known and most clearly remembered facts.

Despite that, or perhaps because of that, there may be instances and incidents where the purist military historian may take issue or find fault with. To my mind, that is okay, since my endeavour is not to delve into strategy, tactics, who was right and who was wrong, but merely to tell the story of a battalion of men at war. A war that none of them wanted. A war thrust upon India by our ever-so-friendly (and oh-so-shortsighted) neighbour to the northwest. A war fought for the sake of yet another neighbour in distress. None of these brave hearts of the Indian Armed Forces were there of their own free will or for personal fame or glory. Many of them did not come back. Many came back, but maimed or with a limb missing. All of them returned with emotional baggage and trauma that they carry to this day, though most would deny that vociferously. I could sense this deep-seated turmoil and see the scars as they narrated their stories. Not many had healed. It took just a few questions for the scab of time to be torn away and the pain to erupt.

And they did all this merely for regimental honour, for the Garud that adorns the flag that they marched under. And for India, of course.

Mukul Deva

PREFACE

Indians, Pakistanis and a host of other military scholars of various hues have written much about the 1971 war. And I am sure much will continue to be written about it. After all, the Lightning Campaign, as the Indo-Pak war of 1971 came to be known, was a landmark in the history of warfare.

Few campaigns in history have caused as much surprise and speculation as the liberation of Bangladesh by the Indian Armed Forces, in 1971. In a mere twelve days, operating over one of the world's most difficult riverine terrains, the Indian Armed Forces brought a formidable, well-equipped and well-entrenched enemy to its knees, took ninety-three thousand Pakistani prisoners and gave the seventy-five million tormented people of Bangladesh their independence.

চিরকাল অটুট থাকবে

Sheikh Mujib-ur-Rehman and Lieutenant Colonel Himmeth – A Farewell to Arms -- Dacca, 12 March 1972 Front page of Bangla Bani dated 13 March 1972

On 12 December 1971, London's *Sunday Times* wrote, '*It took only 12 days for the Indian Army to smash its way to Dacca, an achievement reminiscent of the German blitzkrieg across France in 1940. The strategy was the same: speed, ferocity and flexibility.*'

This is perhaps the only instance where a nation won a war without winning a single major battle. In fact, the war was over before the battles were won. Just as the pride of the German Army stood waiting behind the Defence Wall at Calais when the Allies invaded Normandy and were still intact when the war ended, the bulk of the Pakistani Eastern Army was captured unbloodied.

The Indian aim for this campaign was to install a Bangladeshi interim government in East Pakistani territory before the cessation of hostilities. The problems facing the Indian Army Chief, Sam Manekshaw, were as follows:

1. On the eastern front, enough territory had to be captured to enable the establishment of the Bangladeshi government
2. On the western front, Pakistan had to be denied the capture of any Indian territory, and whatever Pakistani territory could be captured here would help at the negotiating table when the war ended
3. On the Sino-Indian borders, adequate forces had to be maintained. The Chinese were firm allies of Pakistan and had been making threatening noises ever since India was compelled (by the flood of refugees) to intervene in the East Pakistan issue
4. For the campaign to be successful, it had to be swift. India was well aware that the United Nations and the world community, especially America, would mount great pressure, and the Russians had indicated that they did not want to exercise their veto any longer

Pakistani commanders were keenly aware of this basic dynamic. The Pakistanis knew India had been preparing for war for some months, but they were not perturbed. On the contrary, they were confident that a stalemate was all India would be able to achieve. Thus they decided to do the following:

1. Delay the Indian advance into East Pakistan: Hence, the Pakistani Army Commander in the East, Lieutenant General Amir Abdullah Khan Niazi, heavily fortified the towns and approaches to the East Pakistani heartland. He even boasted that should hostilities begin, he would take the battle inside India.
2. Seize strategically important Indian territory on the western front: Hence, Pakistan concentrated virtually all its forces in the West. Their Air Force was equipped with Starfighters, new Chinese F-6s and newer versions of the F-86 Sabre. Their Army had a lot of firepower in the form of heavy artillery, new Chinese built T-59 tanks and US-built Patton tanks.

Keeping in view the geography and terrain of East Pakistan, the brief given by General Manekshaw to the Indian Army Eastern Command was very limited: occupy the Chittagong and Khulna areas of East Pakistan so that an interim Bangladeshi government could be established there. This aim may have been limited; the task confronting the Indian commanders was not.

Three major rivers — the Brahmaputra, the Ganga and the Meghna — divided the then East Pakistan into four natural regions. Each of these rivers was wider than any European river. Each sub-region was further divided into several pockets cut by smaller rivers and their tributaries. The idea that an attacking army could bridge these, get its war machinery across, fight the enemy and then capture territory — all within a couple of weeks — was ludicrous.

The Pakistani Eastern Army was well-entrenched and adequately supplied to fight a defensive battle for months. As was the usual practice with Pakistan, it had diverted the millions of dollars received as aid and for development activity towards building and reinforcing massive defence fortifications on both fronts.

Although the Indian Army headquarters felt they were too ambitious, the Eastern Command went ahead with its plans for a lightning thrust into the then East Pakistan. In November 1971, the Indian Army and the Mukti Bahini guerrillas were ready for battle with the Pakistanis, who were well dug-in and awaiting the Indian assault. The Indian forces outnumbered the Pakistanis by a ratio of about 2:1, although conventional infantry wisdom dictates that an attacking army should have a 3:1 superiority. This, however, was all that could be spared by the Indian Army, considering its other strategic and tactical compulsions.

When all other attempts by India to convince Pakistani to remedy the situation in East Pakistan failed, and India was no longer able to sustain the millions of refugees from the area, war was finally waged on 1 December 1971. Within six days, against all odds, troops of 57 Division (of 4 Corps of the Indian Army) had raced deep into East Pakistan territory. By the seventh day of the war, the Pakistani Army High Command in Rawalpindi was in complete panic. Their border garrisons stood intact and unbloodied as Lieutenant General Sagat, the 4 Corps Commander, spotted an opportunity and decided to exploit it.

The capture of Dacca, which had never been part of the plan, became an irresistible possibility as soon as the Meghna was

Sheikh Mujib-ur-Rehman and Lieutenant Colonel Himmeth reviewing the farewell parade given by 4 Guards

crossed. Soon, the Indian Army had either bypassed Pakistani strong holds or contained them with small forces, and was racing forward towards Dacca at an incredible speed, rivers and terrain notwithstanding.

The day Dacca fell to Indian troops, almost all the heavily fortified Pakistani strong holds in East Pakistan stood intact. Pakistanis were stunned by the speed and momentum of the Indian offensive. They had been beaten: strategically, tactically and psychologically. Their capability to fight had been degraded, and their will to fight decimated.

One of the less remarked upon aspects of the 1971 war was the varied character of the men planning and executing the operations. The best known, of course, was the flamboyant Indian Army Chief, General Sam Manekshaw, who had earlier won the Military Cross in World War II. To the Indian public, Sam, with his twirled moustache, Gurkha cap and baton, was the symbolic hero.

Sam Bahadur with the troops

Yet, below him, there were a few good men who planned and executed their own battles. The Western Army was commanded by Lieutenant General K.P. Candeth, and the Eastern Army by Lieutenant General J.S. Aurora. Lieutenant General Aurora's Chief of Staff was Major General J.F.R. Jacob. Each of them had a major role to play as history unfolded.

Lieutenant General Sagat Singh, PVSM, AVSM, Padma Bhushan. GOC 4 Corps

However, it was Lieutenant General Sagat Singh, General Officer Commanding, 4 Corps, who led the charge and created panic in Pakistani minds by using the forces available to him with ingenuity and courage.

It was Sagat who pulled the plug on the Pakistanis by breaching the Meghna. He made it impossible for General Niazi, the Pakistani Eastern Army Commander, to even consider continuing the battle.

Even less remarked upon is the role played by thousands of unknown Indian soldiers, many of who did not return home to enjoy the fruits of this stupendous victory. Some returned, but not intact. Almost all of them live on or have passed on, unsung and unheard of.

The Garud Strikes acknowledges each and every Indian soldier who took part in this war. However it focusses only on the stories of some of these men—those of the 4 Guards (1 Rajput), and their families.

This book does not, in any manner, wish to undermine the efforts of the other units that took part in this war; nor does it claim that it was 4 Guards alone that turned the tide and won the war. In fact, the story told in these pages could well be that of any of the other Indian Army units that took part in this campaign. Every unit and every man in these units was just one more cog in the wheel that won the war and helped free a nation.

MEETING THE GARUD

There was a familiar jeep waiting for me when I exited the airport. The rising sun lent a strange reddish hue to the gleaming olive green jeep. It immediately brought back memories of the years that I had spent in the olive green uniform.

How many times had such a jeep met me? At countless bus stands, railway stations and airports all over the country. Almost fifteen years had passed since the day I had hung up my boots. But they were swept away in a flash as the impeccably turned out Guards NCO saluted.

'Ram-ram, sahib. Havildar Sachinder Singh, 4 Guards, 1 Rajput, sir. I am your Liaison Officer.' Nothing in his dress or demeanour betrayed the fact that he had driven through the night and been waiting for me at the airport for over three hours now, kind courtesy a delayed flight.

Suddenly I was (almost) ashamed of my baggy T-shirt, faded jeans and shoulder length hair. Reminding myself that I was now an author, and hence allowed a certain artistic licence, I pulled myself together, stiffened the spine, returned his salute, declined the inevitable cup of tea that accompanies such pick-up parties and got into the jeep. We were on our way.

Having been in the air, in the closed confines of an economy class seat, for almost nine hours and on the road for well nigh eighteen, I relished the opportunity to spread my legs. The cool morning breeze slicing in through the open windows more than made up for the lack of an air conditioner. Chiding myself for being a spoilt brat, I leaned back and allowed my mind to rest. It did not take long for me to doze off as we sped through the still deserted roads.

The cry of the sentry bulldozed its way past my layers of sleep. I awoke with a start as the jeep nosed past the quarter guard and halted in front of the 4 Guards officers' mess. Still fighting sleep, I shook hands with the captain, a slim young man, in his mid-twenties, who had been waiting for me at the mess gates.

All vestiges of sleep fell away as two bagpipers burst into music and led the way in; past a huge red banner that proclaimed in flame coloured letters—4 Guards (1 Rajput) 214th Raising Day. Right in the middle of the banner was a golden Garud, upright, with its wings spread wide, grandly and reassuringly looking down at all and sundry, as though to say: its okay… you're on my watch now.

Almost embarrassed, definitely a bit sheepish, I followed suit; it had been a while since I had been exposed to Army ceremonies. Not to mention the fact that, much as I hate to admit it, I had never been in a 214 year old infantry battalion before. Or maybe I had whilst in service, but had never noticed it.

The accumulated weight of all that regimental history slammed into me the minute I set foot inside the officers' mess. There was an avalanche of silver trophies all over the rooms—on the walls, in glass cabinets, on the coffee tables and side tables.

'Most of our silver is still in storage, sir,' my escort remarked with a smile, when I commented on this. 'This is temporary accommodation you see. We don't have much space.' Then, noting my interest, and aware that I was here on an information gathering mission, he led me to a massive trophy in the middle of the room. 'This is our centerpiece, sir. It is…'

Before he could go any further, the Commandant walked in with several other officers and whatever he was going to share with me went unsaid, as pleasantries took over the conversation. However, I was soon to be acquainted with the centerpiece, the very next morning, at the Kasam (oath taking) Parade, which the unit holds every Raising Day.

The mood was sombre when I entered the shamiana (tent) that had been set up on one side of the unit's parade ground. Though I was well in time, almost all the seats were taken. Across the parade ground, directly in front of us, was a huge, newly constructed, gate through which the parade would march in. The guardsmen marshalled on the other side of the wall were not yet visible. However, the unit's colours and their escort, waiting to be marched in, could be seen on our left, towards the far end of the parade ground.

'We are the only battalion in the Commonwealth Nations that has been authorized an extra Junior Commissioned Officer (JCO) to carry our colours,' an old-timer on my left whispered. 'As you know, all Indian Army units carry the President's colours or the regimental colours. However, in the colonial days, the royal regiments had two colours, the regimental ones and either the King's or Queen's colours. In 1858, after the mutiny, our battalion was made a royal unit, the 2nd Queen Victoria's Own Rajput Light Infantry, hence the two colours now. However, in 1805, when serving under General Lord Lake, for the capture of Bharatpur and subsequently Delhi, we were given an honorary colour for exceptional service and one extra JCO was authorized to the battalion for these colours. In 1949, the King's colours were laid to rest in Chetwood Hall, Indian Military Academy (IMA), Dehradun.'

I was still assimilating this when the parade began. There was a strong sense of déjà vu as the regimental colours were marched on. An almost forgotten stirring of once familiar emotions swamped me. In the background, the commentator began narrating the story of the attacks on Delhi, in 1803, and then on Bharatpur, in 1805 and 1824; where the unit got the opportunity to avenge its fallen and regain its honour by capturing the fort that had been denied it earlier. How the regimental colours had been decimated during the first attack, and pieces of it preserved by those who could retrieve them!

I was yet again reminded of how much that simple, metre-long piece of cloth could mean. How willingly men would rally to it and shed blood just to keep that rectangular cloth flying high.

A few minutes later, the parade ground began to echo with several hundred voices, as the men of 4 Guards renewed the oath: to protect and defend the nation and uphold the regiment's honour, no matter what the cost.

The words sounded harsh, the tones gruff, and yet there was something magical in the air; simple, yet incredibly powerful magic. One could sense the passion. And without knowing precisely why, one knew that these were just not words being spouted in some meaningless ceremony. It was evident that these words would be honoured whenever duty came calling. I had experienced such parades before, several times, yet I felt these emotions. It was at that precise moment that I felt connected to this book.

Echoes of the regimental war cry, *Garud ka hoon, bol pyare* (I belong to the Garud, say so, dear friend) reverberated in the parade ground long after the parade had marched out.

An hour later, still feeling all stirred up, I was ensconced in the bachelors' accommodation, waiting for the first of the 1971 veterans to drop in for an interview. Needless to say, I was excited! I was going to hear the story first-hand; from the very people who had swept by the Pakistani garrisons and been the first to enter Dacca. These were the very men who had helped ninety-five million oppressed people throw off a cruel yoke and helped a nation wrest its freedom. I had little idea that the emotional rollercoaster I had been thrown on earlier that morning was still going to grow larger, more real; almost surreal.

Twenty minutes later, there was a grown-up man, well into his sixties, crying unabashedly in front of me, as he narrated and re-lived the story of another who had died in his arms. It is only then that realization actually struck… of what this story meant to those who had lived through those tempestuous days.

One by one they came to tell me their stories; wizened, grizzly, yet incredibly proud—officers, JCOs and Other Ranks—men who had once worn the Garud with a proud flourish. Not even aware that it was they, and men like them, who lent the Garud its sanctity, and not the other way around. Each of them had a story to tell. And they told it simply, and straight from the heart. Without any embellishments, yet fraught with emotions. Pride, grief, fear, honour, anger, and pain: it all came through with startling, heart-rending clarity.

By the time dusk fell, the picture in my head was almost complete. As complete as it could be without the smell of gunsmoke, the thunder of guns, the fear that shrouds every battlefield, and people screaming, bleeding and dying. I felt as though I had been through the war myself, right from Agartala to Dacca; that I knew even those who had either fallen on the battlefield or been taken by time. I was brimming with emotions that I was still unable to pin down or understand fully.

Like many of those old men who told me their stories, that night I, too, cried. An acknowledgement of the feelings those stories had invoked in me. And, for the very first time, as a storyteller, felt the fear that I would not be able to do justice to this book. Though it had been a long and eventful day, sleep wandered nowhere close to me that night.

As I tossed and turned in bed, through the tiny window of my caravan, the brightly lit banner strung across the officers' mess gates caught my eye. The Garud proudly holding its head up in the middle of the banner beckoned me. Like for most Hindus, the Garud is sacred for me, too, kind courtesy its association with Lord Vishnu. However, I had but a hazy idea of why it is so. Unable to resist the sudden urge, I powered up my laptop to find out more. It did not take long for Google to provide the answer.

Kadru and Vinata, the two daughters of King Daksha Prajapati, were married to the great sage Kashyap Muni, who offered a boon to both of them. Kadru asked for a thousand sons and Vinata asked for two, each stronger than her elder sister's thousand. Soon, Kadru laid a thousand eggs and Vinata two. Unable to control her impatience, Vinata broke open one of them to see what was inside. From it emerged a magnificent warrior. However, he was crippled from waist down. He cursed his mother and warned Vinata not to open the second egg before its time, and then rose in the air and went in search of nectar for his thousand stepbrothers. He defeated Brihaspati and the other gods who guarded the nectar and then carried it to Lord Vishnu, the Sun God. Vishnu blessed him to be immortal and invincible in battle. He also appointed him his official carrier. That is how and when the Garud became sacred.

One of the several regimental magazines in my caravan provided the rest of the answer as to why the Garud had been chosen as the regimental emblem by the Brigade of Guards. That came about when General Cariappa accepted the recommendation of senior Guards officers like Lieutenant Colonel Bireshwar Nath and Lieutenant Colonel N.C. Rawlley. In addition to being considered sacred, the considerations were also the elegance, strength, courage and vitality of the great bird. It was for these very reasons that this majestic bird, with spread wings, in standing posture, had been the symbol of the French Army under Napoleon, not to mention the association of the eagle with the glory of the Roman Empire.

These, and a host of related thoughts, were whirling in my dreams that night. Perhaps the supreme confidence of the Garud reached out and touched me, too. Either way, by the time I arose with the morning sun, all my doubts had dissipated. And I knew I could do this book, with no concern for commercial appeal. But only for the feelings of those who had been a part of it.

HOW IT ALL BEGAN

4 Guards (1 Rajput) was carrying out counter-insurgency tasks in the Mizo Hills at the time when Sheikh Mujibur Rehman was arrested, on 25 March 1971. By then, the Mizo terrorists were already on the run and had sought refuge in the Masalang Area, Chittagong Hill tracts of East Pakistan, where the Pakistani Army was providing them active support. Their camps were guarded by a series of Border Out Posts (BOPs) manned by the East Pakistan Rifles (EPR), which mostly comprised Bengalis. During this time, 4 Guards was actively involved in reconnaissance, intelligence gathering and putting together a comprehensive picture of Pakistani interference in India's internal affairs. Soon they began raiding the camps of the Mizo hostiles.

On the very first raid, led by Alpha Company under command Major Chandrakant, some Mizo hostiles were captured. They provided exact locations of key hostile camps and very precise details of Pakistani support being given to them. This concrete and actionable information available now provided an opportunity for India to destroy the Pak-sponsored Mizo insurgent camps and put an end to this menace once and for all. This opportunity became even more real when the Awami League declared independence, and the Bengalis switched allegiance to the new state. This need (to put a final stop to Pakistani support of the insurgency in North-East India and provide depth to the Siliguri corridor) was a major consideration in India's decision to intervene in East Pakistan.

Consequently, the unit was rushed to Agartala. The leading elements of 4 Guards reached Agartala on the evening of 3 April

1971, but before they could go into action, plans were changed, and the orders to search and destroy the Mizo camps across the Indo-Pak border never materialized. Nevertheless, the unit remained in Agartala and thus had a ringside view of the torrid sequence of events that followed in East Pakistan. Not only did they witness the massive influx of millions of refugees into India, they also had a firsthand view of the atrocities that the Pakistan Army inflicted on the people of East Pakistan.

Soon, the trickle of refugees into India had become a deluge. Soon, every possible Indian facility along those borders was swamped. The hospitals were overflowing with men who had had limbs chopped off; women who had been raped, disfigured, and had their breasts cut off. Even children had not been spared. The bestiality displayed by the Pakistan Army cannot be expressed by mere words. Mutilated and mangled, millions flowed into India.

'We were grappling to come to terms with what we saw, as much as we were trying to cope with the daily increasing flood of starving, battered and mutilated people.' The expression on Captain Sutradhar's face conveyed it all. 'I still remember Ted Kennedy standing in the hospital ward when he visited us in July 1971. There was not even an inch of room available in the hospital; every possible corner had been taken up by a mass of humanity … by what had once been normal, happy human beings.' The good doctor was now crying openly.

Ted Kennedy's visit, and the coverage by international media that followed in its run-up, played a major role in highlighting the plight of the East Pakistani refugees and the atrocities committed on them. Till now this was being largely ignored by the American media, primarily because the Vietnam War and the Cold War were at their peak, and America was not very keen to discuss the misdemeanours of Pakistan, its favoured ally in the Southeast Asia Treaty Organization (SEATO) and Central Treaty Organization (CENTO). And also because Nixon and Kissinger were using Yahya Khan to try and effect a rapproachment with China.

The Pakistani Army's atrocities also went unreported because the then UN High Commisioner for Refugees, Prince Sadruddin Aga Khan also happened to be the only child of Sir Sultan Mohammed Shah Aga Khan III, a Pakistani. He allegedly did not hesitate to use his offices to play an ambivalent role and downplay the horrors unleashed by Pakistani soldiers on the hapless East Pakistanis.

'I cannot tell you what terrible things we saw,' Major Chandrakant, then officiating second-in-command and commander of Alpha Company, 4 Guards, muttered bleakly. 'In the months before the war, when we were at Sabrun, every day, Pakistani soldiers would drag naked Bengali (Hindu) women like cattle to the river, right in front of our border outposts (BOPs) and force them to bathe in front of every one ... and they would beat them, rape them and mutiliate them. Those gutless men would even yell at us that this is what the fate of all Indian women would be if India dared to intervene in Pakistan.'

The anguish in his voice was raw even to this day. I tried to visualize what he had described, and failed. My mind could not grasp such a reality. I tried to understand the pain and horror they must have experienced, but in vain. But then I correlated it with the news of the day, where Pakistani soldiers had beheaded an Indian soldier, and I could easily see that the Pakistan Army had lost its soul a long time ago. This is not the way soldiers behave. Warriors the world over live by a code of conduct, and such animal behaviour is not a part of it. There can be little hope for a nation when its Army (its pride and glory) stoops to such bestial behaviour.

'They should not have been allowed to get away with all this. Their officers posted in East Pakistan should have been tried for war crimes, for the sheer bestiality they committed and allowed their men to commit,' Chandrakant's anger was palpable. 'Do you think they would have gotten away scot-free if this had happened in any western country?'

In the face of these continuing horrors, for 4 Guards, the operation to take out the camps of Mizo insurgents now mutated into dealing with the refugees and helping the Mukti Bahini (the East Pakistani freedom fighters) to keep the Pakistani Army at bay and defend the populace of East Pakistan.

However, by virtue of being deployed on the border, 4 Guards gathered important insights into the way the Pakistan Army was functioning in East Pakistan, as well as also learnt a lot about their commanders. These insights were to prove invaluable when hostilities eventually broke out in December 1971.

During these chaotic months, 4 Guards was moving every other day, rushing from one fire to another. 'We must have walked over every inch of the Agartala area,' Major Marwah, who then commanded Charlie Company of 4 Guards, commented, 'sometimes to places so inaccessible that we had to depend exclusively on elephant columns for maintenance.'

By end November 1971, it was clear that war between India and Pakistan could no longer be avoided. The unbelievable burden of millions of refugees on India's economy, the rape of East Pakistan by the Pakistan Army, the exploding aspirations for a life of freedom, equality and dignity of ninety-five million East Pakistanis and Pakistan Army's increasing aggression on both eastern and western fronts made this war inevitable.

Come December, the inevitable came to pass and the Indian Armed Forces moved to rescue a beleaguered neo-nation. 4 Guards spearheaded the Indian Army's advance, right from Agartala to Dacca. Not only did they fight past every obstacle on this incredibly long and difficult road, the guardsmen were also the first to reach Dacca when the Pakistani Army surrendered.

Akhaura, Arahand, Ujjainisar bridge, Sultanpur, Brahmanbaria, Ashuganj, Methikanda, Narsingdi, Lakhiya and finally Dacca. Each of these were unforgettable landmarks on this road. At each of them, many guardsmen shed their blood.

Over forty years have passed since those tumultuous days. The face of the countryside has changed, so much that it is nearly impossible to believe that a deadly war had ravaged it so brutally.

However, sitting with these veterans, pushing through the fog of painful memories, I retraced every inch of this deadly, blood-soaked route. And I felt each and every battle come alive.

THE RACE FOR DACCA

TALLY HO

Several hours had elapsed since they had reached the International Border (IB). And even now no one had a clue if they would be going ahead with the offensive or not; and if so, when.

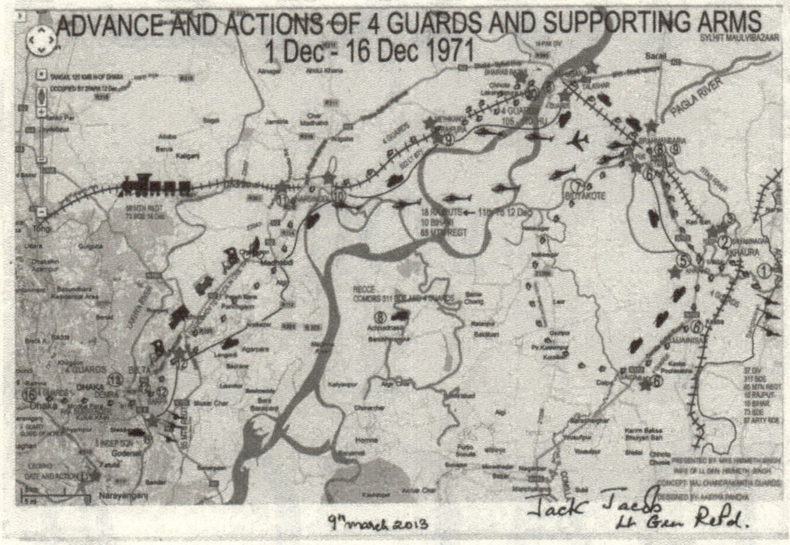

Map signed by Lieutenant General JFR Jacob, PVSM, then Chief of Staff, Eastern Command

However, surprisingly, there was no tension in the air. Most of the men and younger officers had dozed off; exhausted by the intense burst of activity that erupts when any military unit receives the orders to mobilize for war. The others, still riding out the adrenaline surge, and now bored with this lingering inactivity, were trying to sleep. A few were chatting, but in really low tones, mindful of the border outposts not too far away. Some were eating; a very select some... basically the die-hard (and quite literal) followers of Napoleon's an-army-marches-on-its-stomach philosophy.

For the senior lot, of course, it was a different story. Most of them had seen battle before. In the two decades since Indian independence, the country had seen more than its fair share of war, not surprising, considering its unusually belligerent neighbour. This (senior) lot had been through one or more of these wars, and had experienced the terminal impact of bullets, bayonets and bombs on life and limb. They were busy introspecting and contemplating. Perhaps also because the older ones are more prone to thinking and worrying, as are those who command men into battle. Perhaps it was the knowledge of the carnage that was inevitable. Perhaps it was the uncertainty of whether their planning would stand the test of the battle ahead or not. Or perhaps it was simply the certainty that if it did not, their men would pay for the misjudgment with their limbs, and maybe even their lives.

Battalion 'O' Group receiving orders from the Commandant at Agartala on 1 December 1971

Standing (L-R) Captain Harmohinder Singh, Major S. Mehta, Captain V.K. Dewan and Lieutenant Colonel Himmeth Singh

Sitting (L-R) Captain Surinder Singh, Major Kharbanda, Major Marwah and Major Chandrakant

There were over three thousand heavily armed men strung along the border, mostly in small, tight clusters. Barring the occasional man going to discreetly answer nature's call, there was little to give them away.

To mask the movement of these men from the rear areas to the IB, several one tonner trucks had removed their silencers and had been revving their engines to the north of Agartala airport. However, the enemy must have sensed that something was up. It is hard to conceal the movement of so many men. But, the Pakistanis probably didn't know which axis the Indians would exploit, and when the strike would commence.

The sun sets early in this part of the world. Soon it dropped below the horizon and a blanket of darkness rendered even these sporadic movements invisible.

Now cocooned in the fragile shell of darkness, the men of the Indian 311 Mountain Brigade waited… poised on that thin, poorly demarcated line that lay between India and East Pakistan… soon to be Bangladesh.

Commanders (of divisions, brigades, battalions and companies) paced restlessly near telephone sets. The tension coursing through them was directly proportionate to the rank they wore on their shoulder boards. The higher the rank, the heavier the responsibility, and the more fearsome the tension coiling inside them.

Everyone was waiting for two words.

'Tally Ho!'

Two words that would unleash the brigade, along with the other brigades of the 4th Corp of the Indian Army, also poised along the border, and send it hurtling down an uncertain, perilous road, which would eventually lead to Dacca.

Two simple words: that would forever alter the destiny of three nations; one of them yet to be born.

Two tiny words: that would impact the lives of several thousands of men on both sides of the Indo-Pak border.

Two words: the echoes of which would reverberate down the corridors of history forever.

Life, death, the guns, the darkness, the silvery moonlight, even the chill of the winter night: everything seemed to be holding its breath.

At approximately 1730 hours, telephone sets crackled to life.

Tally Ho!

A dozen commanders, scattered in a dozen locations, acknowledged the command. Immediately apprehension, uncertainty and doubt were swept aside as men and machinery rumbled to life, like an ungainly giant uncoiling slowly.

Guns were cocked. Rounds chambered. Bayonets fixed. Boots laced more firmly. Belts tightened. Water swigged to soothe parched throats. Fluttering stomachs settled as adrenaline slithered into the system.

At approximately 1800 hours, the first set of combat boots stepped across the undrawn line of the Assembly Area that had been designated for them and went forward to meet their tryst with destiny.

The date was 1 December 1971.

Once again, Pakistan and India had gone to war.

Lost somewhere in this quagmire of armed men moving forward to engage in battle were the eight hundred plus warriors of 4 Guards (1 Rajput).

Once again they marched under the watchful eye of the Garud.

Battle Ready
The officers of 4 Guards – D- Day, 30 Nov 1971 at Lichibagan, Agartala

Kneeling: 2nd Lieutenant B.B. Midha, Lieutenant Pradhan, Lieutenant Karmarkar, Lieutenant R Mohan (63 Cavalry), 2nd Lieutenant Madappa, Lieutenant Yadav, Captain RAK' Maneck (SIKH LIGHT INFANTRY)

Standing: Captain Sahni, Captain Sutradhar, Major Uppal, Captain V.K. Dewan, Lieutenant Colonel Himmeth Singh, Major S Mehta (63 Cavalry), Major Kharbanda, Major Marwah, Captain Sundaram (Artillery OP), Captain Surinder, Lieutenant L.M. Singh, Major AS Chauhan and Major Chandrakant

Standing at their helm was Lieutenant Colonel Himmeth Singh. Feisty, enigmatic and charismatic; yet for all that a man with all the fears and feelings that all men have.

This is how the strike of the Garud unfolded.

DAY ONE

1 DECEMBER 1971

'To be honest with you, it felt as though we were going for just another training exercise.' Colonel Surinder Singh was returning home early that day and hence he had asked to be interviewed first. And that was the first thing he said to me.

Captain Surinder Singh (Granthi)

Lieutenant Colonel Surinder Singh (Retd.)

We were all sitting in one of the young officers' room. It was not very big; small enough to be really crowded with nine of us in it—eight retired, wizened veterans of the war and me. It looked, felt and even smelt like the typical Army bachelors' quarters: yellow walls, a large part of those adorned with Madonna, Christina Aguilera and the posters of some other strangely done up women I was not familiar with. The aroma of Old Spice after-shave and some other very soothing essence, which I could not identify, mingled with that of the two large dogs sprawled by the bed, an Alsatian and a Golden Retriever. A computer stood in one corner, surrounded by a host of books, on topics as varied and weird as some of the women on the walls.

We were just settling down to begin when the door creaked open and two more veterans walked in. Now the room felt really small. A few minutes passed as I was introduced to the newcomers: Lieutenant Colonels B.B. Midha and A.S. Chouhan.

2nd Lieutenant B.B. Midha

Lieutenant Colonel B.B. Midha (Retd.)

'For so many months now we had been training for this; digging foxholes, man-packing mortars and RCL (Recoilless) guns, moving self-contained for days, and learning to use all modes of transport, mostly improvised. The unit had received almost a hundred new recruits from the Regimental Centre, so there was a lot to be done to get them up to speed. After months of training every day, that is what it felt like when we went across the border that night.'

Major A.S. Chauhan

Colonel Surinder's voice tugged me back. His tone was so matter-of-fact that I was unable to stop my laugh. He did not take umbrage.

'You see, this was my very first time in action. I had never imagined what war would be like, he paused, looking at something in the distance, as though trying to marshal his thoughts, or perhaps recall that feeling. Then he shrugged and nodded, more firmly this time. 'Yes. It felt just like any other exercise.'

A moment later, he added, as though by way of further explanation, 'You must understand, I was a youngster in those days, with barely three years of service. And then, all these months, ever since the problem began in East Pakistan, and refugees began to flood into India, we had been preparing for operations. Every day we would spend hours on the firing range, because our Commandant, Colonel Himmeth Singh, believed that the prime duty of every soldier was to shoot straight. And of course, carry a full battle-load and be able to dig in within minutes. The Old Man laid a lot of stress on this because he had appreciated that in case of any operations in East Pakistan, considering the soft topsoil, artillery would be able to inflict heavy casualties. That is why each of us had to practice digging daily.'

Digging in

'And if you look at the list of people wounded, you will see that's how it turned out eventually. Most of the injuries were splinter wounds caused by the air burst,' he added.

Major Chauhan, then Adm (Administrative) Company Commander, was about to speak when Major Chandrakant pre-empted him: 'In fact Chauhan was one of the first to be hit by an airburst. He had actually been talking to the Commandant when he was hit. This was sometime in July or August 1971.'

Chauhan made a deprecating gesture, but Chandrakant continued: 'I'd like to share something about the airburst. Henry Shrapnel, a Britisher, invented it in 1780, to increase the effectiveness of the canister shot. However, it was the variable time fuse and proximity fuse added to it during the Second World War by the Americans that brought out the true, devilish potential of this weapon. They used it to deadly effect during the Vietnam War. In fact, it is safe to say that it was one of the game changing weapons that turned the tide during the Second World War. They relied on it so much that once, in Europe, the Americans even delayed their advance when the consignment of airburst shells did not reach in time. Now Pakistanis had truckloads of these shells, and used them freely. They were what caused the maximum casualties to Indian troops.'

Major Chandrakant (Paunchy)

Major Chandrakant VrC (Retd.)

I glanced through the 4 Guards casualty list handed over to me by Major V.K. Dewan. 'Splinter Wound' seemed to be the recurring theme in that list. And it was a sadly long list.

I wondered how their Commandant had handled it. Curious, I asked, 'Tell me about Colonel Himmeth Singh.'

'Take a look at this,' Major Chandrakant handed me some papers. 'They will give you a complete idea of what Himmeth was all about.'

I took the papers he was offering me. Right on top were two photographs. The first looked familiar. Then I remembered why; Himmeth's son had shown it to me recently. I also remembered his answer when I had asked him the same question about his father.

'It is hard to talk about one's father,' Mrityunja Singh Ajairajpura, a pilot by profession, who told me he preferred being called Meetu, had replied.

I wondered if he realized he was displaying the same reticence to seek the limelight that his father had been known for.

'The most prominent thing I remember about him was that he taught and led by example. Whether it was helping the servants clear up after a party, or something far deeper, like living within one's means, dad always led the way. All in all, he was a fabulous embodiment of the maxim, "If your father isn't your role model, you're both fixed!" I was really lucky. I don't think any son could have asked for a better role model.'

The words 'role model' struck me. This was the third time in as many days that I had heard Himmeth being referred to as one. First by Brigadier Mac Devaiah, who, as a Captain, had served as Himmeth's ADC (Aide-de-camp). And then, the very next day, by General Shamsher Mehta, who had served with 4 Guards during the war. Unaware of my thoughts, Meetu proceeded.

'The other thing was that he was a very self-effacing man.' Perhaps he realized that was not a very self-effacing statement, and elaborated: 'The best example I can give you is when I was in college and had gone to visit my parents in Dehradun, where dad was posted as the Commandant of the IMA. During my tour of the Chetwood Hall, the curator informed me that father had been the only cadet to have commanded two passing out parades, that of the batch senior to him and his own. Dad never talked about such things. Even when I asked him about it, he casually brushed it aside.'

Lieutenant Colonel Himmeth Singh – Dec '71

'Tell me more,' I prodded, keen to get a picture of the man, not the soldier.

'Just what are you looking for?' Meetu looked puzzled. 'Background stuff?'

'No. That I have. I already know that he was born in June 1928, passed out from the Indian Military Academy with the Sword of Honour, served as an instructor at Infantry School, Mhow, and the Guards Training Centre. I also know that he saw action during the 1962 war with China, had served with the Indian UN Mission in Gaza, and had been an advisor to Emperor Haile Selasie's bodyguards when he was a Lieutnant Colonel before he led the unit through the 1971 Indo-Pak war.'

'That's correct,' Meetu confirmed. 'He also not only commanded a brigade at Fazilka, but also raised a mechanized brigade at Babina, commanded a division at Jammu, and a Corps at Bhatinda.'

Major Chandrakant, who had taken on the role of my shepherd, and been with us that day, too, added, 'Himmeth also served as an instructor at the College of Combat, Mhow and later as its Commandant. He also served as the Commandant of IMA, Dehradun, and National Defence College, Delhi.'

I was already aware of the IMA tenure, since Himmeth had taken over as Commandant just after I had been commissioned from there. It made me wish I'd met him there; I may have had a better idea of the man whose battalion I was writing about today.

'After that,' Meetu concluded, 'in 1987, dad retired. He served for a while as the personal advisor to the then Defence Minister, and subsequently the Emir of Qatar, His Excellency Sheikh Hamad bin Khalifa Al Thani, before he finally hung up his spurs and settled down in Jaipur.'

'Why Jaipur?' I asked, not so much curious as needing a respite, since I was still processing that long and illustrious innings.

'You see, we are from the Rajput house of Ajairajpura. Hence, Rajasthan has always been home for us,' Meetu answered. 'Also, it is from this background that our love for *shikar* and all things martial spring,' he added with a grin.

Having served and been friends with many Rajputs, I understood that. I remember one of them telling me: Once a Rajput, always a Rajput. 'That's the kind of stuff I want to know about him. His personal beliefs, views on religion, etc.'

This time it was Major Chandrakant, also a Rajput, who took up the narration. 'Himmeth had all the required martial blood running in his veins, but he also had a very finely developed sense of values. That is why he never condoned any unsoldierly or cowardly acts like looting or ill-treatment of prisoners. The Old Man was very strict about things like that.'

Now more than ever, I wished I had met the man, and not just because of this book. If everything emerging about Himmeth were true, he would indeed have been a rare man. I now turned to the second photo. This showed the same man, but now with a grizzled beard.

'What's with the beard?' I asked.

'Himmeth was so sure we would win the war that he decided he would shave only when we captured Dacca,' Chandrakant explained, and then laughed. Eager to get the joke I'd obviously missed, I lifted a quizzical eyebrow at him. 'I just remembered what Mrs Himmeth said when she met him immediately after the war.' He laughed again, and explained: 'She said thank god the war only lasted two weeks, else I would have met Rip Van Winkle.'

Lieutenant Colonel
Himmeth Singh – Dec '71

I went back to the papers after we stopped laughing. It was important for me to get a sense of the man who had led the battalion to war.

My eyes again sought out Himmeth's photos as the men around me ran out of words.

Despite having heard so much about him and having gone through the recordings Colonel Pyarelal of USI, Delhi, had made whilst interviewing him, I wish I knew the man better. Perhaps my need was more visible than I realized because Colonel Surinder Singh elaborated.

Lieutenant General
Himmeth Singh PVSM
(Retd).

'Colonel Himmeth was not an easy commanding officer to serve under. He was not only very tough, but also a man with very strong likes and dislikes.' I put down the photos when Colonel Surinder began to speak. 'Why, just yesterday his wife was saying the same thing, that with Himmeth every thing was either black or white.'

'Absolutely true!' Lietenant Colonel Midha chipped in. 'He was full of *josh* and completely focused on whatever he got fixated on, but…' a smile creased his face. 'With him, you were either an angel or a demon; nothing in between.'

'Which were you?' I couldn't help asking.

'A demon, to begin with.' Midha retorted.

This time the laughter took a while to subside.

'That notwithstanding, let me tell you that even today, if I ever have to go into battle again, he is the man I would want us to lead,' Colonel Surinder took over the conversation again. 'Himmeth had tremendous confidence in the *paltan*. And rightly so, since this was the same battalion he had been commissioned in. Did you know that on 1 December 1971, the day we went into attack, he left us free to get things organized and actually went off to play a round of golf,' Colonel Surinder gave a faraway smile. 'Himmeth was a soldier's soldier; tough as nails, but what a charismatic person. Ask Glucose and he will tell…'

'Who is Glucose?' I could not help interrupting.

'I!' Major Dewan, lounging in the far corner, raised a half finger.

Major V.K. Dewan (Glucose)

Major V.K. Dewan (Retd.)

'If anyone knows Himmeth, he does. Glucose was the adjutant back then and with him during the operation, almost every minute right from start to finish,' Colonel Surinder explained.

I had spent a good hour with the gentlemen in question the previous evening, and was unable to correlate the person to the nickname. 'Why on earth did they call you Glucose?'

'Because he was such a Glaxo baby,' Surinder did not wait for Glucose to reply.

Everyone in the room roared with laughter. I threw a quick look around. I am sure they must have heard this story many times before, but they all seemed as engrossed in it as I was.

'All of us had nicknames,' Glucose clarified. 'When I joined the unit, Som ... Colonel Somanna, who had been the Commandant then, gave me two options, Glucose or Glaxo baby,' another loud guffaw, 'and so I obviously opted for Glucose.'

His logic was far from obvious to me, and I was still unclear about the correlation, but fascinated nonetheless. 'And you?' I turned back to Surinder. 'What was your nickname?'

'I was nicknamed Granthi (Sikh religious teacher),' Surinder replied with a naughty grin. 'They called me that because I'm a Sikh, and did not cut my beard and I didn't drink either. So one day, when we were playing football and I missed the ball, Pup Mann (General H.R.S. Mann) yelled at me, "Come on, you *granthi*", and the name just stuck,' he finished, amid laughter.

Looking at the sixty-plus man sitting before me, honestly, it was hard for me to imagine that he had once been young. I struggled momentarily to picture a young captain, improbably and illogically nicknamed Granthi.

'Paunchy. That's me,' Major Chandrakant, tall even while sitting, swarthy, with black, horn-rimmed spectacles that would have been considered nerdy even in the dotcom era, flashed a cheeky smile. 'I always had a paunch, even when I was a cadet.'

'And Tuffy was my nickname,' Major S.P. Marwah gave a broad smile. Looking at the slim, not so tall man seated before me, I had trouble figuring out why they'd given him that nickname.

Major S.P. Marwah (Tuffy)

Major S.P. Marwah SM (Retd.)

I was aware that Army nicknames, though fascinating, are seldom based on anything logical. 'And Colonel Himmeth? What did you guys call him?' I asked.

'Himmeth?' Granthi guffawed. 'Himmeth was Himmeth. Nothing else.'

'No, really, I mean it. Himmeth was just Himmeth. We either called him that, or Old Man, like in the other units.'

I shrugged and gave him a please-go-ahead wave. He started to, but Glucose got in there first.

'Colonel Surinder is right. Himmeth was a tough taskmaster. His fundas in life were very clear. A soldier had to know how to shoot straight and *had* to have the will to win. That's all there was to it, as far as he was concerned.' There was a very short pause. 'In the same way, Himmeth also believed that every officer had to have three things to be a good regimental officer.'

I could not keep down a quizzical eyebrow.

'An officer had to be able to play bridge, play golf, and have a rucksack.'

I understood the fetish about the games; these were common to many Army officers across the world, but the third one went past me. 'Rucksack? What's with the rucksack?' I asked.

'During the months that we were preparing for war, I remember one day Himmeth was returning from his daily round of golf when he saw us practising with the RCL gun.' My rucksack query got swept aside by Lieutenant Colonel Midha. 'We were doing the usual mount-dismount drill, when Himmeth happened to be driving past. He stopped the jeep and gave us a shouting right there and then, telling us to stop the nonsense. He said: "Just make sure that every soldier in your company can point the gun at the enemy tanks, aim it and fire it. That's all that is needed."'

Much as I was relishing this picture of the man who had led the battalion to war, I now felt the urge to get to the war itself.

'So you were saying,' I turned again to Granthi, 'that it felt just like any other exercise.'

'Like he said,' before Granthi could get started, Midha broke in, 'we were all very much in the training mode. So much so that even when we were waiting in the assembly area near the International Border, for the operation to begin, many of us fell asleep.' He looked around at the others for confirmation. 'I know I did. The whole day had been so hectic; gathering our stores, distributing them and the ammunition amongst the men, checking weapons, writing letters to our families, just in case…'

Just in case… The words held my attention. That's how it always is for soldiers, in any uniform, in any country, in any era. Three simple words: *just in case … they never come back*, being the unsaid part of it.

Midha's voice intruded my thoughts. 'There had been a hundred things to do. None of us had slept a wink the past twenty-thirty hours. That is why many of us fell asleep the minute we got to the assembly area,' he said. 'In fact, when we got orders to start the operation, some of us kept on sleeping and so there was considerable confusion. The ones who got up late had lost sight of the men in front and had no idea where to go. It was pretty dark, and visibility was terrible. Himmeth got so mad at Major Kharbanda, our company commander, that he really yelled at him,' he continued.

Naik Hoshiar Singh, the radio operator who had been with Himmeth almost every minute of those sixteen days, must have witnessed the confusion first hand. He was nodding vigorously.

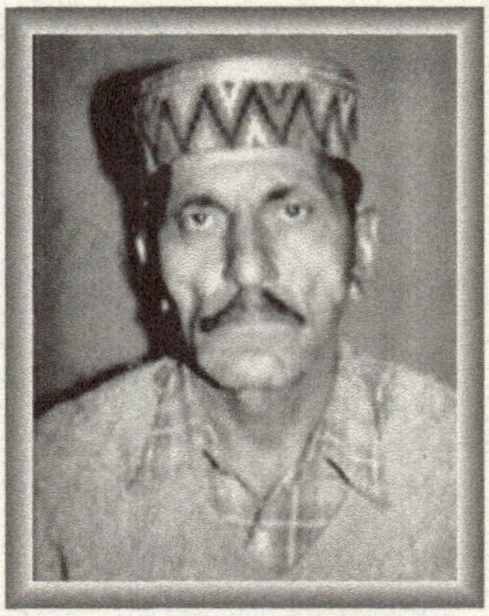

Honorary Captain Subedar Major Hoshiar Singh (Retd.)

'Commandant *sahib* was with the soldiers in front. He ordered them to fire tracer rounds so that the Bravo Company could see them and catch up,' he said.

'Tracers?' I was surprised. 'That must have done wonders to the element of surprise.'

'Surprise?' Midha laughed a very sarcastic laugh. 'What surprise? The Pakistanis had started firing on us almost as soon as we crossed the border. We had barely gone hundred yards when they started off with mortars and artillery.'

'True.' That was Glucose. 'They may not have known what was being thrown at them, but they certainly knew we were up and about. They were holding Akhaura in strength and were very well-prepared to defend.'

The Pakistanis had done their homework. Fields of fire had been carefully worked out and cleared. Artillery and mortars had identified defensive fire tasks along the most likely approaches to Akhaura and were stocked up for an extended engagement. Armour, too, had been sited along tankable approaches. Barbed wire and minefields lay in a deadly ring around Akhaura.

Located almost directly opposite Agartala, the East Pakistani town of Akhaura was an important rail, road and water communication centre close to the Indian border. It was imperative to capture it and secure the area up to the west bank of the Titas river since not only was it the first major hurdle on the road to Dacca, but also because the Pakistani artillery located there was often used to shell Agartala and the Indian BOPs.

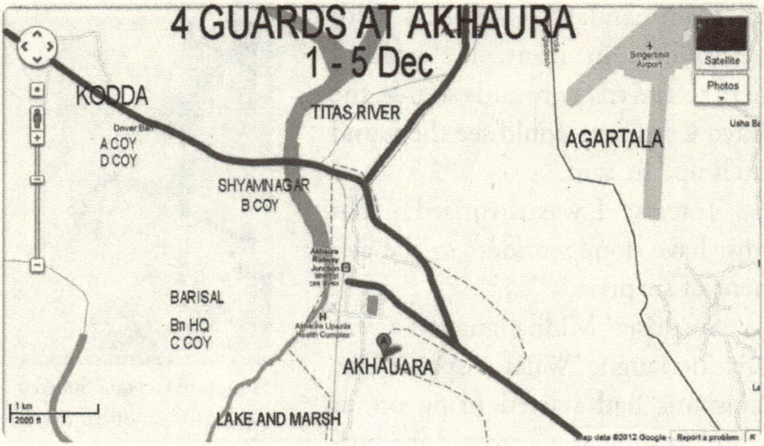

In keeping with the Pakistani High Command's strategy of halting any Indian offensive on the border itself, all major towns and cities on all possible approaches to East Pakistan heartland had been heavily fortified. Each of these towns was very well equipped and stocked to fight a protracted defensive battle, meant to deter and deny the Indian Army from making any territorial gains. Akhaura was one of such strongpoint.

Till such time as the Indian offensive made a breakthrough somewhere, they would not be able to hit the heartland of East Pakistan.

The God of War's arrow had landed on Akhaura. That is where the storm of the Indian offensive would be unleashed first.

That is where the Garud struck first.

The Tripura border is a low lying marshland. The Titas river criss-crosses that particular stretch of land, which the 4 Guards (1 Rajput) would be traversing that night.

There were over eight hundred of them present in the battalion on that day. And each one of them was aware that there was a strong possibility that they may not return alive from this foray. Or maybe they would, but without an arm or a leg. However, whatever apprehensions may have nestled in their hearts, there was only firm resolve on their faces. This, after all, was the day that they had been groomed and trained for. This, after all, is the *raison d'etre* of every soldier; to live with honour and, if required, to die with dignity. But, in either case, ensure that the mission is completed.

The gravity of the occasion may not have yet sunk in, but the enormity of the task facing them began to, within minutes of crossing the border.

'The original plan had been for our battalion to capture Akhaura with a frontal attack,' Granthi leaned forward and pointed it out on the map spread on the bed between us. 'We had planned everything accordingly. We had even carried out the recce and all.'

'4 Guards, along with a squadron of tanks, was given this task,' Paunchy elaborated. 'We were to carry out the attack with three companies and the tanks from the south, and the fourth company, mine, was to infiltrate behind Akhaura and set up a block to cut it off.'

'All the while, this is what we had been planning for,' Midha interjected. 'I remember my company commander, Major Kharbanda, going on recce twice with an armoured corps officer, Lieutenant Mohan, to check the terrain and the infiltration routes. Kharbanda was one of Himmeth's demons and always got selected for such tasks,' continued Paunchy amid loud guffaws from everyone. 'Every time he had to go across, he would hand over his ring and rudraksh etc. to me, along with several instructions, just in case he didn't come back.'

'Even though the terrain helped, the patrolling was a pain,' Glucose pointed out. 'Luckily, we had very confident Bengali guides, the Mukti Bahini chaps.'

'They were okay,' Granthi sounded dubious. 'Major Kharbanda always said he could never be sure how much we could rely on them once the guns opened up. Once that happened, it was anyone's guess if they would stay or run. But in those days, before the war, they were pretty useful. Each company had ten Mukti Bahini men allotted to it, though we had managed some more on our own. Our people would dress up as civilians and go through the enemy lines with them.'

'Yes, Major Kharbanda used to really crib about that,' said Midha again. 'He used to say that he looked like a Bengali when he wore civilian clothes.' Again, there was no malice or bias in his tone, just good old, rustic North Indian humour.

'Bravo Company commanded by Kharbanda and my company (Alpha) would be leading the advance, which is why we were landed this task. Kharbanda was the obvious choice for the recce patrol as he originally came from Dera Ismail Khan, and could speak Pushto. Thus, in the event of being accosted by the enemy, he could bluff his way out by masquerading as a Pathan, or so we hoped,' he explained further.

It sounded hilarious now. I wondered what Kharbanda would have had to say about it back then.

'I didn't want to go since I was also the 2IC (second-in-command) and knew the detailed operational plan. I was worried that if I got caught, they would hammer the plan out of me,' Paunchy pointed out sheepishly.

'The terrain did facilitate patrolling, but it would make operations really painful, especially since we did not even have maps of the area across the IB,' Glucose added. 'Luckily, Paunchy had managed to get hold of an old 1963 survey map of that region from Major Zia Ur Rehman.'

'And who was he?' I asked, as the plethora of unfamiliar names was becoming confusing.

'Major Zia was an East Pakistani officer who defected. He came to us on 10 April 1971 and operated from our location for three months.'

Major I.P. Kharbanda VrC

'He used to chat with us often.' Guardsman Islam Mohammed of Alpha Company added. 'When he found out I was a Muslim he asked me if we (Muslims) faced any problems in the Indian Army. When I explained to him that our unit was a mixed class one and had a fair number of Muslims and Christians, he was quite surprised. Even more when I shared that no one cared about our religion as long as we did our duty.'

Though Islam was tucked away in a corner, perhaps overwhelmed by the abundance of officers and JCOs around, his mammoth moustache made its presence felt. 'You've always had that?' I asked.

'This?' He grinned and gave it a stylish twirl. 'It used to be much better. When I joined the unit in 1966 Colonel Somanna was the commandant and Major Muthanna was the 2IC. Both had *huge* moustaches and all of us used to try and copy them... so everyone was either wearing a Somanna cut or a Muthanna cut.'

Wishing I could have seen both styles, I asked. 'Why was Major Zia surprised?'

'He said they had been told in the Pakistan Army that India did not respect or value Muslims.' Islam explained. 'He was amazed how all of us mingled and lived together in complete harmony.'

'Right.' This was fascinating stuff, but wanting to get back to the war, I turned back to Paunchy. 'You were saying...'

'He later on became the Chief of Army Staff of Bangladesh under Mujib-ur-Rehman. Subsequently, he went on to become the President of Bangladesh till he was assassinated, and his widow replaced him,' Paunchy explained. 'Zia had brought several Pakistani maps with him, and on one of these we found an old footpath that skirted around the Pakistani positions at Akhaura.'

Himmeth was intrigued when Paunchy showed him the path on the map. They realized that the path would most likely be underwater during the monsoons, but probably usable otherwise. In either case, it was worth exploring and Himmeth told Paunchy to do so, since by now it was clear that the battalion would be playing some role in the investment of Akhaura, as and when operations were launched into East Pakistan.

Paunchy was pondering how best to do that when fortune presented a strange solution.

The Agartala airfield lay right along the International Border (IB) and was often used by Indian Army officers to eyeball the area across. It was on one such mission, to study the lay of the land across the IB, that Paunchy ran into Captain Gogna, an Air OP (Observation Post) officer.

'I think it was towards the end of July 1971. Gogna was not only my coursemate from NDA, but we were both from Juliet Squadron, and good friends, too. Gogna, who later retired as a Brigadier, was flying Alouette helicopters for the Air OP at that time. When I shared my predicament with Gogna, he happily agreed to take me up for a joyride, so that I could carry out an aerial recon of Akhaura,' Paunchy went on explaining.

Half an hour later, the two Juliet Squadron coursemates were airborne. Though not really equipped for an aerial recon, Paunchy managed to eyeball Akhaura properly, and even spotted a ditch-cum-bund (DCB) that the Pakistanis had built between Akhaura and Agartala airfield. Thoroughly enthused, Paunchy returned to the airfield the next day, armed with binoculars and a map, and went up again with Gogna.

'It was during this recce that I was not only able to get a good idea of the Pakistani defences, but also realized that they were greater in strength and were far better organized than what had been initially appreciated by us,' Paunchy added.

'What had been the initial appreciation?' I couldn't help asking.

'That Akhaura was held by an infantry company or so.'

When Paunchy returned with this information to Himmeth, he was very excited and also expressed a desire to carry out an aerial recon. He even wanted the other officers to do so. Consequently, that evening found Paunchy back at the airfield looking for Gogna, 'but this time I took Tuffy along for moral support.

He was also our coursemate, and I was a little worried that Gogna might think we were really piling on.'

But Paunchy's apprehension proved unfounded. So strong is the NDA bond and *espirit de corps* that Gogna could scarcely refuse. He happily agreed to take Himmeth and the other officers up for a spin one by one.

'The Old Man was very enthused and we started sending all the unit officers one by one,' Paunchy laughed.

Gogna's air taxi soon became so popular that by the time his flight was rotated out from Agartala a few weeks later, one by one, not only did all the 4 Guards officers get an aerial view of Akhaura, but also many of the brigade officers, including Brigadier Mishra, the Commander, had been on the trip. Not only that, due to Brigadier Mishra's insistence, even the other battalion commanders had enjoyed the pleasures of the Akhaura excursion.

'As luck would have it, Gogna's flight was replaced by a flight of Krishak aircraft, one of which was being flown by Bhargava, also from NDA and only one course senior to me,' Paunchy's face suddenly fell. 'It is unfortunate that Bhargava is no more, but he was a gem, and continued the excellent work Gogna had started for us.' Then, surprisingly, he laughed. 'Bhargava was a real character. One day he even suggested to me that we should carry hand grenades to throw down at the Pakistani positions in Akhaura.' He saw the query glinting in my eye and added: 'Of course I did no such thing. The Old Man would have thrown a fit.' Some fond memory made him laugh again. 'By now our recon flights were no longer casual affairs. We maintained proper logs of each flight, made markings on our maps, and meticulously studied the ground in and around Akhaura.'

By a strange quirk of fate, the only one who did not manage to eyeball Akhuara from the air was Himmeth; something or the other always came in the way. However, luckily, with the help of all these air recons and ground patrolling, supported by intel reports, it was soon clear that Akhaura was defended by 12 Frontier Force Rifles (FFR), along with elements of 33 Baluch, 12 Azad

Kashmir (AK), some tanks, artillery and an extensive minefield. In keeping with its strategic and tactical importance, Akhaura was a formidable obstacle.

Glucose, the perennial adjutant, did a swift tally to check if they had missed anything. Having ensured we hadn't, he moved on. 'That's why, on the night of 23rd or 24th November, when Lieutenant General Jagjit Singh Aurora landed up at the brigade headquarters, our orders were changed. Now, Akhaura became an investment by the division. Two battalions would attack it, a third would go behind to cut if off, and other units would carry out feints and diversionary attacks,' said Glucose, swivelling the map towards me again. 'A frontal attack by a battalion would have been crazy.'

'As reported by Paunchy, the Pakistanis had also dug a massive anti-tank ditch across the complete frontage,' Lieutenant Raj Mohan of 5 Independant Armoured Sqaudron pointed it out on the map. 'That is why the brigade attack had to go in from the flank.'

2nd Lieutenant Rajendra Mohan

Major Rajendra Mohan (Retd.)

As per the new plan, 4 Guards was tasked to go behind Akhaura from the west and take up position astride the Brahmanbaria-Akhaura railway line. They had to cut Akhaura off and ensure it could not be reinforced.

'I am sure the Pakistanis did not anticipate this,' Glucose gave a grim grin. 'I don't think they would ever have imagined that an entire battalion of eight hundred men could wade through the swampy, marshy river with over five feet deep water.'

'It was that bad?' I queried.

'Worse!' Tuffy replied. 'Everything got messed up. We were soaking wet. Everything was covered in mud. Our weapons got clogged, everything got thoroughly soaked and all the food we had been carrying was ruined. We were wet and cold and it felt as though we had crawled through from some really slimy ditch.'

'During our earlier stint in the Mizo Hills, we had suffered this problem of barrels getting clogged with mud and then either bulging or exploding when the weapon was fired. Anticipating this, we had decided to take some prophylactic measures,' Tuffy's mischievous grin should have given me an idea of what Paunchy was implying. 'The RMO (Regimental Medical Officer), Captain Sutradhar, told me how horrified the other doctors at the hospital had been when he requisitioned a thousand condoms.' There was a loud burst of laughter. 'Sutradhar had a tough time explaining that the condoms would be used to protect rifle barrels from getting mud clogged.'

I tried to imagine the scene—hundreds of men, toting condom-clad rifles, wading through waist deep mud. I guess one has to actually go through it for the mind to be able to conjure up the real picture. I gave up as Paunchy resumed.

'Let me tell you the plan in detail first. 10 Bihar was supposed to lead upto Lonesar, make a lodgement there for us (4 Guards) to move forward, infiltrate through enemy lines and cut off Akhaura from the west. Once it had been isolated, 10 Bihar was to attack Akhaura, whilst 18 Rajput, the brigade reserve, stood by to exploit their success or reinforce the attack, whatever was required. To confuse the enemy, 12 Kumaon had to simultaneously launch a feint attack on Akhaura from the east, and 19 Bihar, along with 12 EBR (East Bengal Regiment), from the north.'

Glucose added, 'In terms of armour, the 5th Independent Armoured Squadron was grouped with us. One of their troops would support the attack by 10 Bihar and the rest of the squadron was to come with us.'

As he spoke, Granthi helpfully pointed out the various approaches to me on the map. It was not a military grade map, but the story unfolding through the eyes of this motley crew was clear enough. 'Some of us were pretty cut up with the General for changing our original orders; which were, that the attack had to be carried out only by 311 Mountain Brigade. This was an audacious plan. It had an element of surprise in timing and direction of the attack. If successful, it could possibly have ensured speedy capture of Akhaura.' Granthi was now sombre. 'Lieutenant General Aurora, however, took a more cautious approach and changed the plan to an investment of Akhaura by 311 Mountain Brigade with an element of 73 Brigade in a supporting role. As things turned out, it was not a bad decision since the Pakistanis were well dug in and a frontal attack by the battalion would have been nothing short of suicidal. But back then, the issue was that many of us, especially the junior lot, did not know why the plans had been changed.'

By now, memories seemed to flowing thick and fast.

'Sometime around last light on 01 December 1971, I think it was at about 1800 hours, we all moved out,' Tuffy reflected for a moment, as though trying to ensure he got the details right. 'As Colonel Surinder said, it was like going out for just another exercise. One didn't really feel anything. Not yet anyway. That would come later, when the Pakistanis started shelling us. At the time we started out, it was all very confusing, and there was a feeling of numbness,' he said.

On their backs, the guardsmen had as much ammunition as they could carry, and also three days of packed rations. If what I sensed in them even now were any indication, in their minds would have hovered the fog of uncertainty that every battle brings with it. And of course, the fear, which even the bravest of the brave feel. And rightly so, for that is what keeps one alive in the battlefield. That is what spurs us on to attempt the impossible.

However, knowing what they accomplished in the coming days, in their hearts would surely have burned the need to prove worthy of the Garud they marched under.

'10 Bihar was leading the initial infiltration up to Lonesar, a little south of Akhaura,' Granthi added to the sketch earlier made. 'After making contact with the enemy, they were also supposed to find a gap in the southern defences so that 4 Guards could infiltrate ahead and cut off Akhaura from the west.'

Despite the passage of four decades, the words were flowing seamlessly. It was easy to tell that they all had re-lived these moments several times before. Having been in combat myself, I could empathize with that. Such memories don't go away easily. They come back many times in the silence of the nights, mostly as nightmares that jolt you awake and leave you sweating.

The Pakistanis defending Akhuaura started shelling as soon as Indian troops crossed the International Border. By the time 4 Guards reached Lonesar, a little short of Devagram village, Pakistani shelling had become intense.

'The enemy must have obviously detected our movement. Their artillery fire grew heavier with every passing moment,' Granthi seemed lost. 'I cannot tell you what it was like. The first to cut and run were the civilian porters who were helping us carry ammunition. Each company had been given ten of the Mukti Bahini men as porters and guides. They took off as soon as the firing started. In the process, we lost a fair bit of ammunition.'

Lieutenant Colonel A.S. Chauhan now spoke for the first time.

One of the first Emergency Commissioned Officers, Chauhan had been a police inspector with the Madhya Pradesh police in his previous *avatar*. Thus, relatively older than the other officers, and far more experienced, the younger lot looked up to him. Even today, This was visible.

In the wake of the guardsmen, Chauhan was moving forward with the Rajputs, along with a platoon of Mukti Bahini boys, ferrying ammunition and rations forward when the shelling started.

Before the second salvo could hit, the Bahini boys had run, scattering into the night.

Having suffered a leg injury earlier that year due to an air burst splinter, while serving as a platoon commander with Charlie Company, Himmeth had tasked Chauhan to take over the duties of Adm Company Commander. It was his job to ensure the boys did not run out of ammunition, food and water. To Chauhan's credit, before long he had been ordered to command the Brigade B-echelon.

'I was amazed at the speed with which they all vanished,' a wry smile twisted across Chauhan's face. 'One minute they were moving with us and then, the very next minute, there was just my JCO and a couple of our boys left standing there. Some of the Mukti Bahini boys had dropped the ammunition they were carrying, but a lot of them had just run off with it,' he added after a moment. 'It was unfair to blame them; they were young, completely unfamiliar with the grim realities of a battlefield and scared of the horrors they would suffer at the hands of the Pakistan Army should India fail to win the war,' he elaborated.

Chauhan was also aware that there was no way he could not get the ammunition and food up to the boys. So, even though he was unable to bend his knee due to the injury, and regardless of the pounding being meted out by the Pakistani artillery, he went hunting for the missing porters.

'I sent the JCO in one direction and went into the other myself,' he said.

The Mukti Bahini boys had taken shelter either in the buildings around or in the jungles. Literally dragging them back, Chauhan and his JCO finally got most of them together again and resumed their trudge forward.

'I must confess their flight also disheartened a few of my own boys. But, despite everything—mud, slush, enemy fire—we carried on regardless,' he added. The pause this time was longer. I could sense Granthi's fight to regain control of whatever that had been unleashed in his head by those memories. 'Even today I can see their artillery shells exploding all around us. I can still smell the gunpowder. I can still see the fiery sparks spray out into the air every time a shell burst. Soon, very soon, we would smell the blood, as they began to take a toll,' he voiced his thoughts.

Granthi had gone very still. So had the rest. I was the only one in the room who had not been there that night. I was the odd man out; the others were all lost in their thoughts. 'The exercise ended at that moment,' Granthi's volume had dropped considerably, almost a whisper now. '*That* is when the war became real. Real and bloody.'

He paused again, shook himself slightly, as though trying to get rid of some troubling memories. Then the soldier's stoicism, and that strange sense of humour, which keeps them alive and ticking, kicked in, almost on cue, knowing it was required to lighten the burden ... and the moment.

'You know a very funny thing had happened earlier that evening. I was the Support (SP) Company Commander at that time, and just before we started, Himmeth told me that I should be ready to take over from whichever rifle company commander fell first. He told me that in front of all four of the rifle company commanders. I still remember Paunchy telling me not to dare to even dream of coming to take over Alpha Company, which he was commanding, even though I had been commissioned in it. Immediately, Major Kharbanda, who was commanding Bravo Company, also told me that he would not let me come to Bravo either. Tuffy, who was commanding Charlie Company, told me that my aspirations of commanding his company would never materialize. That is when Major Vijay Uppal, who was commanding Delta Company, gave me a pat and told me that since I did not seem to have much choice left, I should feel free to come to his company whenever I wanted to,' Granthi elaborated.

He was no longer smiling now. No one in the room was. 'It was strange since it was Uppal who fell first. He took a splinter, from an artillery air burst, in his upper leg, in the groin area. It was a really bad one and he went down immediately. Barely an hour after we were launched, Himmeth ordered me to move forward and replace him as Delta Company Commander.'

The silence was absolute. The sound of a jeep engine revving somewhere outside intruded. Then even that died away. The war had entered the room now. Real. Stark. First blood had been drawn.

Lieutenant Raj Mohan was moving with Himmeth and the battalion 'O' group. They were coming up to Devagram village when they encountered a huge front of sharpened *panjee* (sharpened bamboo stakes); very much like those that had once guarded the moats of medieval forts. Or the implacable wall of spears of a Roman phalanx.

Bravo Company, commanded by Major Kharbanda, was leading the advance for 4 Guards. They halted and began to scout a way around the *panjee*. That is when the first salvo of artillery shells found them. They were airbursts, lighting up the night sky sporadically, like giant firecrackers. Obviously, the guardsmen had blundered down one of the defensive fire tasks selected by the Pakistani defenders of Akhaura.

'The guardsmen were all carrying picks and shovels. They went into the digging mode immediately,' Mohan gave a rueful grin. 'We (tank-men) had none so we just hugged the ground.'

The second salvo was much closer; almost directly overhead, as though the Pakistani Artillery OP (Observation Post) had corrected the range.

'I heard Major Uppal cry out. He was just a yard or so to my right. He was screaming and seemed to be in tremendous pain,' Mohan added.

Vijay Uppal felt a sharp blow smash into his lower body. Initially, there was no pain because the high velocity impact of the splinter numbed the flesh. Then pain surged through him like a never-ending wave. Moments later, he felt someone kneel over him. Despite hot lead churning all around them, the medics went to work, trying to staunch the bleeding and stabilize him. Gentle hands began to seek and dress the wound.

'When I reached Uppal, he was screaming in pain,' said Paunchy. 'Vijay Uppal joined 4 Guards when we were at NEFA (North East Frontier Agency) in the early part of 1971. He was an EME (Electrical and Mechanical Engineering) officer on attachment to our unit.'

I noticed the last bit came out a bit condescendingly and was unable to stop my smile; *some things never change.*

For the uninitiated, a word about the caste system that afflicts armies the world over is important. Fighting arms (like the infantry and armour) look down on the supporting services (like the EME, ASC and AOC). Although, being a good old infantryman myself, I must add that I have always wondered why they include armour in the fighting arms. They do little by way of fighting, so I guess it must be because of all the sound and fury they generate when they move… or should that be *if* they move.

The artillery firing grew heavier and more accurate as Pakistani gunners corrected the range. Raj Mohan struggled to hug the ground closer. It was a while before the firing eased a bit. The guardsmen seized the moment and began to move again. The medics loaded Uppal on a stretcher and began to cart him away, back towards the Advanced Dressing Station (ADS). When Raj Mohan got up, he realized that the stitching on the rear of his pants had ripped open: 'I was feeling terrible! I borrowed a piece of my tank driver's *pagri* (turban), and wrapped it around my waist.'

Feeling a little better with his modesty now partially restored, Raj Mohan resumed his march forward with Himmeth's group.

But it was with a delicate, slighty twisted walk that he went forward to Akhaura, and the battle for it, which was now to commence in all seriousness.

Despite their best efforts, 10 Bihar was unable to locate a suitable gap in the Pakistani defences for 4 Guards to infiltrate through at Lonesar. Time was running short. As per the plan, if 4 Guards had not started infiltration by midnight, then the unit would not move ahead to encircle Akhaura from the west.

The operational window was closing fast when Brigadier R.N. Mishra, Commander, 311 Mountain Brigade, arrived on the scene.

Brigadier R.N. Mishra VrC

Brigadier R.N. Mishra VrC (Retd.)

In the midst of gunsmoke and confusion, no one noticed the curtains fall on the first day of December, and a new day began. With it came a deep, rolling fog, settling down on the warring men like a cold shroud.

'The fog was heaven sent. It prevented the enemy from really getting a fix on us, especially our numbers,' Granthi explained. 'And, of course, when daylight came, it was the fog that kept us alive.'

DAY TWO

02 DECEMBER 1971

At the stroke of midnight began the assault on Akhaura. Signaling the start was a barrage of covering fire by the Indian artillery.

'I don't think I will ever forget that sight—of about fifty artillery guns of our division firing simultaneously on Akhaura. We were about two or three kilometres away, but even at that distance we could feel the earth shake, and the sky was torn apart by sheets of lightening,' Paunchy's tone was tinged with awe. 'It was one long roll of thunder. I am not sure how long it lasted, perhaps fifteen or twenty minutes, but it seemed to go on forever.'

'True,' concurred Tuffy Marwah. 'I had no idea what damage it caused to the Pakistani defences at Akhaura, but it was one huge shot in the arm for our morale.'

The Pakistanis were not sitting quietly either. By now, their artillery was blasting the attacking forces with everything in their arsenal. There was a blanket of gunpowder and smoke over the area. Adding to the disorientation of the men was the nerve-shattering thunder of exploding airbursts.

'By now all our senses seemed to have gone numb,' Granthi mused. 'One could see everything, hear everything, smell everything, but as though from far away. Yet, it was all horribly real.'

Brigadier Mishra walked into this hellfire, accompanied by his IO (Intelligence Officer), radio operator and the usual protection detail, not that they could have done anything to protect him from the death that was raining down from the skies.

'The Old Man always said that we were damn lucky we had gone to war with a commander like Mishra,' Tuffy reminisced. 'A simple, god fearing man, Mishra was from a renowned family; his father had served on Lord Mountbatten's staff. The commander was polite to a fault, except when he had to lay down the law, or when one failed to live up to his expectations. His most endearing quality was that he was extraordinarily humane.' Tuffy leaned forward, to emphasize his point. 'Right from the word go, the commander was with us, literally. We were waiting for 10 Bihar to find a gap for us when he landed up.'

Along with the rest of the unit, Himmeth had also gone to ground and was waiting for the go ahead from 10 Bihar. Seeing the brigade commander sauntering around as though he was out for a morning walk, Himmeth went up to him and advised him that it would be safer for him to take shelter behind the embankment in the rice field.

'Later, the Old Man told me what Brigadier Mishra's reply was: "Himmeth, Pakistanis have yet to make the bullet that will kill me. I am going to retire peacefully and die only when my time comes… from natural causes",' Paunchy had a faraway look in his eyes as he narrated this. 'And how right he was… Brigadier Mishra is still around, happily retired and living a peaceful life.' Then, returning to the moment, he looked at me. 'Brigadier Mishra was present with us at every decisive moment, at every crucial point in our headlong dash for Dacca. So much so that after the war, when we were going through a de-briefing in the brigade headquarters, and there was some acrimony between the battalion commanders regarding the battle for Ashuganj, Mishra intervened and took the blame. He had said "Perhaps I got too involved with the 4 Guards heliborne operations across the Meghna. I should have been with the bulk of my brigade, fighting the battle at Ashuganj.",' said Paunchy. 'Such honesty and sense of responsibility is rare. It takes a big man to stand up and take blame.'

Declining to take shelter, Mishra heard out Himmeth's briefing patiently and realized that there was an acute danger of the brigade's operation getting stalled.

Unwilling to allow that to happen, Mishra immediately went ahead with his Intelligence Officer and one of the 10 Bihar company commanders.

Perhaps fortune does favour the brave. Perhaps the presence of so senior an officer in their midst spurred 10 Bihar to try harder. Either way, a gap had soon been found.

However, by now it was 0200 hours, almost two hours after the designated time by which they had to begin infiltration. Any later than that and the guardsmen would face a major problem; since the sun comes up rather early in Bangladesh, and the distance to be covered by 4 Guards was such that the battalion would most certainly be hit by day light before they could reach their destination behind Akhaura and dig in.

Mishra, a veteran of every battle the Indian Army had been involved in since Independence, knew what that meant. He had commanded a battalion at Thanga during the 1962 War, and then another one in J&K during the 1965 operations, where he had won a Vir Chakra. Caught out in the open, almost four kilometres deep inside enemy terrirtory, the guardsmen would be sitting ducks for Pakistani guns, artillery and aircraft. But Mishra also knew that the Rubicon had been crossed, and pulling back would not have been a very palatable option. Having been commissioned in 1 Rajput himself, Mishra knew what the unit was capable of. However, he was also clear that he would leave the choice to Himmeth. 'You now have two hours less to reach your objective. Still want to go ahead, Himmeth?'

The Brigadier may as well not have bothered to ask. Himmeth accepted without hesitation. Regardless of the hot lead flying all around, 4 Guards got up and began to cross through the gap in enemy defences.

By now there was no hiding from the Pakistani garrison the fact that the enemy was afoot. Though the Pakistanis could not have yet known the size or intention of the Indian troops moving past, they obviously knew that something was coming at Akhaura and they must have sensed something big was going down. Almost on cue, the firing intensified. And if the air was thick with artillery shrapnel, the ground below was doing the Indians no favours either.

Literally wading through waist deep slush, the guardsmen slogged ahead. The ground was treacherously soft and soggy. It offered no purchase, and sometimes the slush and water was neck-deep.

'Even worse, the slush sucked in our feet and clung to us with the tenacity of a leech. From Lonesar onwards, there were places where the damn marsh was neck deep,' Midha winced, the memory now fresh again. 'Every step forward was a real battle.'

Perhaps the going was even tougher than usual, since none of them had any illusions about what lay ahead. First light was barely three hours away by now. With it, the enemy fire would not only intensify, it would even become more accurate. With first light would also come the Pakistani Air Force and tanks. Both would be able to take on the Indian troops more effectively.

The enemy Air Force was a battle beyond Himmeth and he left it to the Indian Air Force to take care of it. However, the Pakistani tanks were a major cause of worry. Himmeth knew that without their RCLs, his men would be hard pressed to keep the tanks at bay. Each rifle company had one 3.7-inch Rocket Launcher; they provided some solace. However, they were of World War II vintage, and their accuracy and efficacy to beat back enemy armour was questionable.

The RCL guns were not faring well at all. The 106 RCL is normally carried mounted on a jeep; however there was no way a jeep could navigate this terrain. Realising the difficulty of trying to man-pack or bicycle-carry them through the slush and marsh, Himmeth had ordered two RCL guns (with their ammunition) to be carried on top of the squadron of PT 76 tanks, which were accompanying 4 Guards. However, things had gone horribly wrong right from the start.

The troop leader Lieutenant Mohan was one of the officers who had carried out the ground recce with Kharbanda, and confirmed that the PT76 tanks would be able to navigate the route they had selected. Either he had allowed hope to override reason, or had been too troubled to realise that amphibious tanks can swim across water, not mud. The soft, soggy and sticky slush was way beyond the capability of the tanks to navigate across.

'It was so scary. Every time the tanks went up an incline or came down a slope, we were falling all over the place. The guns and ammunition had been lashed on to the tanks, but we were simply clutching on for dear life,' Havildar Mukund Singh Hira, who, along with Havildar Shiv Taj, had been tasked to get the guns up to the forward companies, said grimly. 'None of us had ridden on top of tanks before.'

It was easy to sense that the night had not gone well for him. The tall, dark and gaunt Sikh from Ludhiana sitting in front of me seemed the kind who took life as jovially as possible, but right now he was in a sombre mood.

Honorary Captain
Mukund Singh Hira

'The *paltan* (battalion) had left at around five or six pm, but we left Litchi Bagan much later. In fact, it was around midnight when we finally crossed the border. It is impossible to tell you how much slush there was. We were surprised that the *paltan* had managed to get through all this. It was terrible. The tanks were barely moving. We were struggling to inch forward, one of them getting stuck literally every few metres. And there was so much of fog we could hardly see anything,' he added.

Mukund Singh's brow was knitted in concentration, and his voice had acquired the slow, yet steady, cadence of a man who was watching a film unfold in his mind's eye. 'Now I cannot imagine how we kept going. And then, just when we thought things could get no worse, enemy artillery started up and kept getting more intense and accurate with every passing hour. Then came daylight, and with it came the Pakistani Air Force. They would have had no trouble spotting the stranded tanks because they attacked immediately.'

Naib Subedar Shiv Taj, one of the other Non-Commissioned Officers (NCOs) with the RCL team, ordered them to get off the tanks and dig in. Every guardsman was carrying small shovels and picks, and began to dig in.

By now the fog had lifted and it was broad daylight. The Pakistanis were attacking the Indians with all their might: mortars, artillery and every now and then their aircrafts would attack. Barely able to move in the slush, the tanks were sitting ducks, but luckily they all made it through. Either the Pakistani pilots were not too good, or they were afraid to come lower and attack. But it was still horrible sitting through all that.

'We were huddled together in the mud when we got orders to take Major Uppal back. He had been hit by splinters from the artillery airbursts and was in bad shape,' Mukund looked a trifle dazed.

'Was he conscious?' I could not help asking.

'Oh yes, he was,' Mukund replied grimly, 'and he must have been in tremendous pain. He kept yelling at us to move carefully, but the ground was so slippery and there was so much firing that we had to keep putting him down every now and then. And every time we did that, with every jerk he would yell and curse. Somehow, we got him back and handed him over to the administrative party behind us and then returned to the tanks and tried to move ahead again.'

By now the rest of the battalion was well over two kilometres ahead of the tanks. They had barely managed to get moving when they hit a nallah. It was not very wide, but the banks were so slippery that the tanks simply could not move. The tracks were not getting any purchase on the ground and they started slipping and sliding.

Up ahead, the rifles companies of 4 Guards were not faring any better either, with the Pakistanis laying down a deadly curtain of fire on them.

With the skies raining death and the ground sucking them down, every step was excruciatingly slow and painful. Despite all this, the Gods of War seemed to have been watching over the guardsmen that day.

When the first streaks of dawn stained that death-laden night, it brought with it a thick blanket of fog. Visibility was barely a few yards, at times so terrible that it was hard to see the man in front. Probably that is why, despite having started out two hours later than planned, the battalion managed to get into position unseen by the enemy. Not that the Pakistanis stopped firing. But there is no doubt that their fire would have claimed many more casualties had the guardsmen been visible in daylight.

By 0700 hours, on 2 December 1971, the unit had reached Barisal. The battalion headquarters deployed there along with C Company. And the other three rifle companies took off for their objectives. A Company was to secure and deploy at Kodda, B Company at Shyam Nagar, and D Company was to take Chandi.

'We were still a couple of kilometres short of Shyamnagar when we were day lighted. It was near about six or six-thirty in the morning. Right in front of us was the Titas river. There was not much water in it, but the riverbed and area around was very slushy and marshy. And across the river, about a hundred and fifty metres from us was the Akhaura railway station,' Lieutenant

Colonel B.B. Midha now took over the narrative. 'Bravo was leading since the Company Commander Major Kharbanda had been on recce several times over this area and knew it very well. Now we were following precisely the route that he and the guides had reconnoitered. '

'What was your rank and task then?' I asked, quite overwhelmed by the relentless barrage of information being thrown at me while I was still trying to sort out the basics.

'I was then a Second Lieutenant, a platoon commander in Bravo Company. I had joined the unit just a few months ago,' he said, as a smile creased his face as memories assailed him. 'You know, when I was commissioned from the Officers' Training Academy (OTA), I did not even know where 4 Guards was. They thought the unit was in Assam and I was given a railway warrant up to Amguri. When I reached there, no one seemed to have any idea where the *paltan* was. So finally, using civil transport I managed to make my way to the Mariami transit camp, about sixty kilometres away. The Officer Commanding (OC) was a fine guy. He also had no clue where the unit was, but told me to relax, and said they would find me. It took seven days but they did. The unit, which was actually in Aizwal, sent some men to pick me up from Silchar; that was the nearest railway station.'

Midha gave an apologetic look, probably aware that he had meandered away from the war.

'While on that journey, I realized that 4 Guards was very well known. Firstly, because it was a very old unit, and secondly, because Lieutenant General Sagat Singh, the 4 Corps Commander, had a lot of respect for our Commandant, Himmeth. They had probably served together for a while in the Infantry School. Anyway, as I mentioned earlier, within a couple of hours of reaching the *paltan*, I had landed on Himmeth's demon's list.' There was no rancour in his grin. 'But not for long. As the war clouds gathered, Himmeth began to focus on junior officers a lot. It was a major change that we all noticed. He would give us a lot of attention and often used to say that it was the young officers who were going to win the war for us. In those months, he put all of us through massive training. I remember, one day my company threw over four hundred grenades.'

I was impressed.

'In Himmeth's dictionary, a soldier had to have two things: the ability to shoot straight, and the will to win. According to him, everything else was pointless,' Midha paused; as much for a sip of tea as to streamline his thoughts. 'So that day, on the morning of 2nd December, we were still a couple of clicks short of our objective, Shyamnagar, when daylight found us. Major Kharbanda told us to go to ground. We were not very sure where the Pakistanis were, and probably that is why Kharbanda was reluctant to move once the visibility improved. Everyone was relieved to get the load off their feet, since by now, we had covered four or five kilometres, most of it through horrible slush. But when Himmeth came to know that we had stopped, he was very upset at Kharbanda and gave him a piece of his mind on the radio. Very soon, we got moving again. Luckily, the fog had come down again so we could move undetected. However, by the time we hit the Titas river, the fog had lifted again and there was no way we could go ahead. Anyway, there wasn't much ahead to go to,' Midha concluded, as he leaned forward to show it to me on the map.

'We found ourselves barely a hundred and fifty metres from the Akhaura railway station when the fog finally lifted. Naib Subedar Dhura Ram, whose platoon was leading the advance, thought there was some movement ahead, just past the railway station, and so we went to ground again. It may sound funny now, but we were all still in the training mode, even after all that artillery shelling the whole night. Or perhaps our minds had just gone numb. Everyone was so uptight about weapons, magazines, binoculars and everything else. That is when I realized I had lost one of my magazines. Major Kharbanda made us all check our controlled stores, and we found that several other men had also lost their magazines. It must have happened while we had been wading through the slush. Major Kharbanda was very upset, considering he had recently been admonished by Himmeth and the effect was still fresh,' Midha recounted with relish. 'He told me to go with Subedar Bikker's platoon and see if there was a Pakistani post ahead. He actually said, "I don't care if you find the post or not, but just get hold of some Pakistani magazines."'

'You're kidding, right?' I was incredulous.

'I'm serious,' continued Midha. 'How do I explain? We had been so focussed on keeping our equipment secure during training, that it had gotten ingrained in our heads.'

'So did you go and get the magazines?' I asked.

'Obviously! We started out towards the railway station... Bikker and I. We'd gone about a hundred metres when artillery fire intensified. It was so heavy that we had no chance of moving forward at all. We were wondering what to do when, luckily, Major Kharbanda called us back,' his smile was gone now.

'It was only then, when people started dying, that we realized this was no training exercise. We realized that the Pakistanis were actually deployed in a part of the railway station. There were a handful of Pakistani Razakars firmed in on the western bank of the Titas river, defending Shyamnagar,' Midha elaborated.

Bravo Company began to dig in, knowing that they would be sitting ducks for the Pakistanis who were in proper field fortifications, literally within touching range.

The Pakistanis had spotted some movement and had called for speculative artillery fire, but they were still not completely aware of the full extent of the threat. Due to the fog, they were unaware that the enemy was already at their doorstep.

'I think they confused us, either with the Mukti Bahini, or a commando raiding party, or a patrol... I'm not sure, but...' Midha broke off as his thoughts scattered momentarily.

After a while, the artillery fire petered off and activity on the Pakistani post increased as visibility normalized.

No matter what the circumstances, men will be men and bodily functions do exert their inherent pressures. Answering to one such pressure, unaware of the guardsmen deployed yards away, several Pakistani Razakars headed across the railway tracks with their bottles of water, straight towards Bravo company. A few of them died before the others spotted the trenches that Bravo had dug, and that is when they realized how close the Indians were.

'I can never forget the sight of that Frontier Force officer... He was a young, handsome chap, lying dead in the field with a water bottle beside him,' Midha mused.

That is when reality bit for the Pakistani defenders securing the railway station. Within minutes, hell erupted all around Bravo. Dhura Ram's platoon, which was right up front, closest to the enemy, bore the brunt of it.

Artillery began raining down on them, as did a host of machine guns and small arms. If anyone in Bravo had still harboured any doubts about being in a training exercise, those doubts died a rapid death then. The war had come home for Bravo Company!

The Pakistanis must have noted the heaps of freshly dug mud that had suddenly sprouted in front of them. The freshly dug mud piled up in front of the foxholes provided excellent aiming marks for the Pakistani Razakars.

'I can't tell you how many slugs I found in the mud pile in front of my trench,' Midha gave an inadvertent shudder. 'The firing was so accurate that we could not even raise our heads. We knew we had to prevent the Pakistanis from bringing down aimed fire on us. Major Kharbanda asked Captain K.S. Sundaram, the Artillery OP deployed with us, to do the needful.'

Sundaram was unable to direct fire from where he was pinned down. Braving heavy automatic fire Sundaram moved to a hut about a hundred metres to one flank. The Pakistani machine guns harried his operator and him every inch of the way, but he made it across and started to engage the enemy defences.

'But his luck did not hold out for long. Moments later, even as he was directing artillery fire, a Medium Machine Gun (MMG) burst found him,' Midha's tone was grave. 'He took a bullet smack in the head. He didn't have a chance! Neither did the man next to him. A couple of others were also injured.'

Casualties mounted and the situation rapidly grew precarious for Bravo Company. So little was the gap between the Indian and Pakistani trenches that even the Pakistani 2-inch mortars were proving to be deadly accurate.

'It was only then, when people started dying all around us, that we realised that lost magazines and all meant nothing… That we were really at war,' Midha added, a near whisper.

There was one particular machine gun that was making life really difficult for Bravo. Not only was the gun well sited, it was also manned by a very accurate gunner. Desperate to either destroy the machine gunner or at least force him to keep his head down, Kharbanda ordered Midha to take over Sundaram's radio set and direct the artillery fire.

'I only had a general idea of how to do that, but I must have done something right because the very first salvo was almost on target. It overshot the target by barely hundred metres,' Midha's tension was palpable in his voice even now. 'But then, in all the confusion, I forgot that we had already crossed behind Akhaura and were now facing India, hence our artillery guns were in front of me, not behind me. So by mistake, I told them to add hundred, instead of asking them to subtract hundred. That almost got all of us killed. Another fifty metres, and the shells would have landed right on our heads. Major Kharbanda almost killed me,' a tight smile indicated how severe the rebuking from Kharbanda must have been.

Just then, the rumble of tanks was heard. By now, they all knew that their own tanks were stuck way back, so it could only be the Pakistani tanks coming up. The sound was still some distance away, but growing louder by the minute, approaching rapidly.

Tension soared as Bravo steeled itself to meet the onslaught. However, though they did not know it yet, it would be their neighbours, Alpha Company, who were going to bear the brunt of the Pakistani armoured ire.

'My company reached Kodda by 0700 hours on 2nd December. It was daylight already, but visibility was almost nil due to a thick fog. That was good for us, otherwise the Pakistani Artillery OP's would have wreaked havoc on us,' narrated Paunchy, who'd been commanding Alpha Company. 'Despite the safety blanket of the fog, the last few hours had been hellish. It is funny now when one thinks of it, but I can clearly remember when we had been back in our base and I had been giving orders for our task to my company 'O' group. It had all seemed so simple then. Kodda was a nice little dot on the map, about five kilometres inside enemy territory, beckoning us. And the Titas river just a lovely blue line wavering curvaceously across the terrain. It had no water, no slush! It was just a wavy blue line, not at all daunting.'

He lapsed into silence as his mind went back to all those years, and to that tiny, unremarkable company command post in some now forgotten, unmarked place along the border. I found myself holding my breath, scared to do anything that might disrupt his march down memory lane.

Half of Alpha Company had already crossed Kodda, a longish village. Paunchy was halfway through the village when they spotted a Pakistani Razakkar. He was even more startled than they were. Then the Razakkar tried to make a run for it, but one of the guardsmen tripped him and he went down sprawling. Realizing that they could not be far from the main Pakistani position, and would be in serious trouble if the enemy soldier raised an alarm, Paunchy pushed his gun barrel into the man's chest and shot him. The muffled shot went unheard by the Pakistani defenders.

Paunchy's laugh was mixed; part upset, part bewilderment. Perhaps still stunned by the ease with which he had killed another human being.

It is not as though any of the commanders had underestimated the problem of getting eight hundred plus men, in full battle gear, with their arms, ammunition and a dozen other things that an Army carries into battle, across the Titas.

'How are we going to cross the river, sahib?' guardsman Veer Singh of Alpha Company had been forthright enough to ask his Company Commander.

Paunchy gave a wry laugh. 'Veer didn't realize that his guess was as good as mine. Plans made in the sanctuary of the operations room seem so simple and do-able. But walking the talk?' He gave me a level look. 'The entire operation of finding a gap in the enemy defences, then going around their defences, deep into enemy territory, and then clearing some well planned defences and finally taking up position, with the enemy swarming all around us…' he broke off with another half-laugh. 'While giving orders, it had all been summed up in one simple statement — encircle Akhaura and establish a block at Kodda. When you put it like that, it sounds so simple, doesn't it,' he shrugged. 'I guess it is what it is!'

Paunchy was savvy enough to know that much would depend not just on the answer he gave to Veer Singh, but the confidence and panache with which he gave it. 'We will swim across it, of course,' he had replied, his tone ringing with the confidence that has been the hallmark of guardsmen down the ages. Nothing in his tone communicated even an iota of the apprehension that was coursing through him. He had studied and reconnoitered the river in detail, and knew that getting a combat-ready company across it was going to be a monumental task.

Fully loaded, each man would be toting fifty-plus kilograms on his person. The battle-load (of ammunition, rations and other essential supplies) constituted another several tons. All of this had to be taken across the river. The country boats or streamers that normally ran ferry across the river were under the control of the Pakistani Army. The folding boats available to the Indian troops could be used to ferry only a part of the most critical ammunition and supplies.

Adding to the complexity was the fact that the entire operation had to be carried out under cover of darkness; and therefore time was seriously short, since the sun rises early in this, the eastern part of the subcontinent.

And of course, all this would be done under the merciless shadow of the enemy's guns.

But Paunchy, like the others, was also aware that no matter what the odds, it had to be done. There was no choice. It was now no longer just a task, but a matter of regimental izzat or honour. No shame could be allowed to fall on the Garud.

If Veer Singh was taken aback or amused by the answer, he hid it well. With ten years of service under this belt, and a hundred years of Guards' tradition in his heart, Veer Singh was also fully aware that his apprehensions and anxiety would be contagious. He knew that he had to stand by his Company Commander and show conviction in his decision by taking the lead himself. Which is why, when they hit the edge of the river, Veer Singh was the first man from his platoon to enter the water.

The water was freezing and the river was shrouded with a thick layer of mist, reducing visibility to a few measly feet. Of course, just hours later, this same mist would prove to be their saving grace, by preventing the Pakistanis from bringing down aimed fire on them. But that was later. Right now it made the going miserable.

'Within minutes, everything had gone numb,' Paunchy mused. 'We went in cold and numb and came out muddy, wet and even more numb.'

Not the most glorious of starts for a war that history would later remember as one of the greatest military victories for the Indian Army.

'War can be a real bitch,' Paunchy remarked in a solemn, understated manner.

Granthi arrived in Delta Company and took charge within minutes of Major Vijay Uppal being evacuated. The loss of their commander and the spate of casualties so early in the game had dampened the morale of the company. It had also ignited a lot of anger, and the men were eager to avenge their fallen comrades.

Despite their best efforts, Delta Company was unable to infiltrate across to Chandi, their objective, since the Pakistanis were holding a position enroute.

'We were going along when suddenly I saw a man in front of me. For a second, I thought he was one of ours. I then realized it was a Pakistani soldier. He was right there, in my face, barely a few feet away,' Granthi looked equally surprised.

The Pakistani was shocked by the group of men who erupted out of the fog suddenly. He had been on Listening Post (LP) duty with another of his comrades.

'Obviously they had not been taking their task seriously or they would have heard us coming. Even his rifle was lying on the ground about five feet away from him. He ran for the rifle but one of my havaldars shot him,' Granthi said as a matter of fact. 'The second man on LP duty with him must have gone around the corner or something. Perhaps he heard the shot and ran away, because we never came across him.'

Delta Company continued probing ahead in the fog. Almost immediately, they ran into another Pakistani post.

'It seemed to be a small one,' Granthi explained. 'We could hear them talking to each other and could make out that there were not too many of them.'

Captain Maninder, the Delta Company 2IC, who was with the leading platoon, called out, asking the Pakistanis to surrender.

'I heard them hurl abuses in reply,' Granthi gave a mischevious grin. 'They were also speaking in Punjabi.'

In addition to abusing them, the Pakistanis must have also called for artillery support because minutes later, Delta Company ran into a renewed hailstorm of artillery fire. Amongst those wounded was the company 2IC, the enterprising young Captain Maninder.

By now, daylight was already upon them. And the fog too had started thinning out. It would not be long before the fog dissipated completely, leaving the guardsmen without cover, and exposed. Unable to move ahead to Chandi, Granthi conferred with Paunchy.

'The artillery fire was pretty accurate despite the fog. I realized it would be suicidal for Delta Company to try and cross the five hundred odd metres of open ground, which lay between us and Chandi, so I told Granthi to dig in behind my company, till such time as the Old Man fetched up and we figured out what to do next,' Paunchy said.

The two were conferring when they heard the rumbling of tanks, a sound dreaded by every infantryman, especially those whose anti-tank weapons have yet to fetch up. Delta Company frantically began to dig in.

Alpha Company had barely gone fifty metres from the place where Paunchy had shot the Razakar when they stumbled into the schoolyard at Kodda. Mustering there were a group of Pakistani Razakars, perhaps for the morning report.

'My olive green uniform had by now turned khaki with all the mud, so they must have mistaken me for one of their officers, because one of them, perhaps an NCO, marched up to give me the report. My men had also come up to the schoolyard and we surrounded them. We immediately disarmed the whole lot, but then not knowing what to do with them, since we had no resources to take them prisoners, I told them to run away. They did, pretty eagerly,' Paunchy grinned.

By now the fog had started to lift, and the leading elements of Alpha Company had made contact with the main Pakistani position at Kodda. There were some enemy soldiers defending the small bridge on the Akhaura-Brahmanbaria railway track and some more on the bigger bridge.

Paunchy knew how important the bridges were. Crucial, since the railway line formed the vital link between Akhaura and Brahmanbaria. The Pakistanis were also using the railway embankment as a road; it was elevated, level and firm enough for their vehicles.

The Titas river flowing alongside was yet another critical communication artery for the movement of troops and supplies. So getting control of these bridges would not only enable the Indian forces to dominate all three of the communication channels and cut off the defenders, but also allow the Indian Army to move their administrative echelons forward far more easily. That was imperative for any sustainable operation in the heartland.

The Pakistanis, as yet, seemed unaware that the Indians had closed in so much, and in such strength. Perhaps that is why their response had so far been largely restricted to defensive artillery fire. Alpha Company immediately went to ground.

'Intelligence had told us that there were about twenty to twenty-three Razakars guarding the small bridge, and a section of Pakistani regulars supported by some more Razakars securing the bigger bridge,' said Paunchy. 'However, there were many more. In fact, eventually we took close to two hundred Razakars as prisoners at Kodda that day.'

Tasking Number Three platoon, commanded by Naib Subedar Desraj, to clear and secure the smaller bridge, Paunchy headed for the bigger bridge, about seven hundred metres to the east, with the rest of the Company.

Naik Ram Khilawan Singh, an ex-mortar man, and now the Commander of Number One Section, was one of the first men to reach the bridge. With the element of surprise on their side, the guardsmen soon had the bridge under their control. The handful of Razakars who did not fall to the guns of the guardsmen fled after a cursory resistance.

Desraj rapidly deployed two sections of his platoon on the eastern side of the embankment, towards Kodda, and his third section on the western side of the embankment, so that it could dominate the river.

'I was in the process of preparing Defensive Fire (DF) task tables when I suddenly saw a train with three bogies pulling out from Akhaura railway station. It was heading for Brahmanbaria,' Captain Mahipal Singh, who was the artillery OP with Desraj's platoon, said.

Captain Mahipal Singh, Artillery OP

Major General Mahipal Singh VSM

Comfortably attired in a white cotton shirt, the now retired Major General Mahipal Singh was looking cool and relaxed in his Chandigarh home. 'My first impression was that the Pakistanis at Akhaura were still not aware of our presence, or the fact that we had taken over the smaller bridge already.'

That illusion was soon shattered as the train came to a halt right in the middle of Desraj's platoon, neatly separating the two elements of the platoon. Now they began to rain down automatic fire from all three bogies on the guardsmen caught on either side of the embankment.

Caught out in the open, the platoon began to take casualties. In the very first few minutes, Iqbal, the radio operator with Mahipal Singh, lost his life. Enemy fire also took out both the radio sets with Singh.

'Even otherwise, I could not have engaged the train with artillery, since our men were on either side of it. We were too close together,' Singh looked grim. 'Desraj extricated the section on the western side through a culvert in the embankment, and that made things a little better. But the loss of both my radio sets was a big blow and seriously handicapped my ability to provide fire support.'

Paunchy, with the rest of the Company, was about half a kilometre away when he heard the firing. Seeing his platoon in trouble, he stopped immediately and began to provide whatever fire support he could.

'But there wasn't much we could do; the enemy and my boys were so closely intermingled that it would have been impossible not to hit some of my own guys,' said Paunchy, with a regretful tone. 'But we did manage to fire the RL (Rocket Launcher) at the railway wagons.'

That convinced the Pakistanis in the train to pull back into the railway station. With that crisis momentarily resolved, Paunchy resumed advance on the bigger bridge.

'That's when we realized that the Intelligence guys had messed up, since the bigger bridge was actually held by a Company of Pakistani regulars.' Paunchy gave an exasperated headshake. 'We had been told it was only a handful of Razakars.'

Aware that it was beyond their capability to take this bridge on their own, Paunchy decided to pull back and build up on Desraj's platoon, which by now had deployed on the smaller bridge and was consolidating its position. They were still some distance away when Pakistani artillery began blasting Desraj's platoon. The Company halted again, unable to proceed till the artillery fire had abated a bit. However, there was to be no respite. Following hard in the wake of an intense bombardment, the Pakistanis counter attacked the third platoon with an infantry company and a troop of PT 76 tanks.

Unwilling to give the Indians time to consolidate their position on the bridge, the General Staff Officer Grade 1 (GSO-1) of the 14th Pakistani Infantry Division, an armoured corps officer, had quickly marshalled a mixed bag of troops and led the attack on Desraj's platoon.

'We were unaware that the Pakistanis were holding these PT 76 tanks. We learnt later that five of them had been given to Pakistan by Indonesia,' Paunchy explained. 'Initially, when we saw the tanks approaching, I thought they were ours, since the armoured squadron supporting us was also using the PT 76. It is only when they started firing that we realized they were enemy tanks.'

With the Indian armour supporting 4 Guards and the RCL guns still stuck in the slush and marsh enroute, Desraj's platoon had little to blunt the Pakistani counter attack with.

'To make matters worse, the artillery OP deployed with that platoon, Captain Mahipal Singh, had lost his operator and radio sets in enemy shelling. They could not even call for artillery support to break up the Pakistani assault,' Paunchy's anguish was obvious. 'By now we had also lost the 3.7 inch RL man, so Desraj's platoon was completely at the mercy of the Pakistani armour.'

Now totally unsupported, with its back to the wall, the platoon fought back tooth and nail, trying to hold out till the rest of the company fetched up. But the pressure was immense, men were falling like ninepins now, and the platoon was inexorably driven back by the Pakistani tanks.

Lance Naik Lakhpat Singh saw the shattered remains of his section trying to extricate as the nearest enemy tank closed in on them. He must have known his Light Machine Gun (LMG) would not have any effect on the tank, yet hoping to provide his comrades with a window of opportunity that would allow them to escape, he kept firing. The last sight Lakhpat saw was a Pakistani tank bearing down on him.

Naik Ram Khilawan Singh saw Lakhpat ground to dust as the tank's tracks churned over him. Having been in battle myself, it was easy to understand that by now blood lust would have swamped all vestiges of reason. Racing forward, he went for the tank with nothing but a grenade and will power.

'I saw Ram Khilawan jump on top of the tank and actually punch one of the Pakistani soldiers. Himmeth had come up to my location and was with me at that time. Even he saw the whole incident.' There was awe in Paunchy's tone. 'What Ram Khilawan did was absolutely amazing. He must have known he would not survive that attack.'

Ram Khilawan did not. Neither did the Pakistani tank.

Paunchy, still struggling to fight his way through to his beleaguered platoon, also saw Lance Naik Pirabhu Singh go down.

The loss of every man is a knife in the heart of every commander. In the case of Pirabhu, it was more so, perhaps because Pirabhu, a loyal and caring Jat from Hissar had been by Paunchy's side for many years. As Paunchy's batman, Pirabhu had literally been his shadow. The two had been so close that when, earlier that year, Pirabhu had passed the promotion cadre and been promoted to Lance Naik, Paunchy had gifted him with an HMT watch, an expensive and treasured item in those days, even for an officer.

Paunchy was boiling with rage as he saw his platoon being shredded into pieces, but he knew he was still too far away. He could see his men fighting back valiantly. And he could see them falling like chaff before a threshing machine as enemy tanks thundered over the trenches. Here and there, he could see his men being hauled out of trenches by Pakistani soldiers, and being clubbed and shot down in cold blood.

'I could not stop myself.' Paunchy was shaking with anger. 'The brutal manner in which the Pakistanis were gunning down even wounded men was too much. I ordered my Medium Machine Gun (MMG) to open fire, even though the Pakistanis and the men from my own platoon were too closely intermingled. I knew that some of my own men would also get hit, but by now it was clear that the enemy would not let them live in any case.'

The MMG fire accounted for several Pakistani soldiers. However, I did not see any satisfaction on Paunchy's face as he narrated that. Whatever satisfaction it may have given him had been drowned by the sorrow of seeing his men also mowed down.

Despite such raw courage, Desraj's platoon was fighting a losing battle and trying hard to extricate from that impossible position. Superior numbers and the Pakistani tanks soon overran the platoon.

By the time Number Three Platoon finally managed to extricate itself, it had been decimated by almost half its numbers. Despite their best efforts to get their dead and wounded back, the bodies of seven of the men lay where they fell. Fallen, but not forgotten.

Captain Mahipal Singh, the artillery OP, managed to crawl back to safety with the shattered remanants of Desraj's platoon. He was doing so when an enemy artillery shell landed almost beside him.

'Himmeth was with me at that time. We both saw the shell land almost on top of Mahipal and the handful of men crawling back towards us. We were pretty sure they were all gone, but when the dust and smoke cleared,' there was disbelief all over Paunchy's face, 'we saw that they were still coming towards us.'

Luckily, the ground was soft and the shell buried itself in, sufficiently deep for it to leave Mahipal, and the others around him, unscathed. Not one of them so much as got a scratch.

Like every other man in the company, Paunchy knew he would not leave the bodies of his men behind. But in that moment, he was desperate to stabilize the situation. He was also clearly aware that his options were limited, and falling back was not one of them. There was no back to fall upon. After all, when you infiltrate behind enemy lines and cut off the enemy, you also get automatically cut off from your base. Alpha Company knew they had to stand and fight. They began to dig in.

'There were four engineer men, six anti-tank mines and about as many American manufactured M14 jumping mines with us. I ordered these to be planted on the main approach that led to where I had deployed the rest of my company. There was a clear path leading up to our position. It lay between two water tanks,' Paunchy drew a rough sketch to help me get a clearer picture. 'The water tanks were about twenty feet by twenty feet in size, and offered some kind of an anti-tank obstacle. I hoped they would funnel the Pakistani tanks into the open patch between them.'

However, the Pakistani tanks now decided to attack the guardsmen through Kodda village. Alpha Company saw the tanks come rumbling through the villages, knocking down the huts. There was nothing that could stop them overrunning the infantrymen caught out in the open.

'That was the first time I felt real fear,' and it was still audible in Paunchy's hushed tone. 'Seeing those monstrous things coming at us, and knowing that we had nothing in our arsenal to stop them. I'm not afraid to admit it: I was petrified.' He gave a slow headshake. 'But I also knew that I was the Company Commander, and every man would be looking up to me to lead by example.' He halted. 'It was a matter of honour … regimental izzat … you know how it is… officers are not allowed to show fear. Well, somehow, neither did I.' There was a much longer pause. 'We held our ground.'

The five Pakistani tanks closed in slowly but surely. The menacing roar of tank engines escalated as they closed in, till they were about seventy-five metres short of the first foxholes of Alpha Company.

'They now halted and kept revving their engines, as though to scare us off. However, for some reason, they did not fire their main guns at us. Nor did they complete their attack on our position. Perhaps if they had realized how tenuous our position was, they might have moved in and finished us off.' Paunchy's relief was evident.

Witnessing the ongoing battle from close quarters, Himmeth knew he had to reinforce Alpha Company or risk losing most of it. Getting on to his radio set, he ordered Delta Company, deployed just behind Alpha, to move forward and build up on Kodda.

Meanwhile, the sounds of the Pakistanis coming up again were increasing and Paunchy sensed they would be under attack again soon. He somehow managed to re-group and deploy the remaining two platoons rapidly.

'Desraj's platoon took seventeen casualties… almost half its strength,' Paunchy tried to stay matter of fact, but his anger was palpable. 'We were not sure but we had a feeling that a couple of boys had been taken captive.'

In all the confusion and scramble, they had no time to worry about the dead or send out search parties to look for those missing.

Amongst those captured by the Pakistanis at Kodda was Guardsman Jameel Mohammed of Alpha Company. No Indian soldier captured by the Pakistanis had it easy. The wounded received no medical aid. Many were mutilated and brutalized before they were killed. And if the bodies of the soldiers of 10 Bihar found later by Paunchy at Brahmanbaria were any indication, the dead received no burial or cremation. However, for Guardsman Jameel Mohammed, life proved exceptionally hard when he fell into the enemy hands.

When the Pakistanis found out that he was a Muslim, they tortured him brutally for supporting the *kafir* (infidel) Indians against them.

Of the seven guardsmen of Alpha Company captured at Kodda, Jameel was selected for special treatment and beaten up really badly.

'The one inadvertent fallout of his capture was that whilst interrogating him, the Pakistanis learnt that 4 Guards (1 Rajput) was part of the Indian attacking forces,' Glucose interjected. 'General Niazi, the Pakistani Eastern Army Commander, had earlier served in the ranks in 1 Rajput. When he learnt about our unit, he asked for all captured guardsmen to be taken to Dacca for interrogation. That perhaps was the only reason that some of our men did not meet the usual fate of any Indian soldier taken prisoner by the Pakistanis—a bullet in the head.'

By now, the condition of several of the casualties was deteriorating fast and the unit medics were constantly in action, more often than not treating the wounded under artillery fire. The RMO, Captain (Dr.) H.P. Sutradhar, who incidentally had graduated from the Dacca Medical College, was a harried man.

'We had barely travelled a couple of miles when Sutra told me that he had lost his carbine,' Glucose gave a grim laugh. 'The poor guy had been so busy rushing from one casualty to the other that he had no idea where or when he dropped it. Not that I could imagine him firing a shot even in anger.'

Sutra tasked Lance Naik Bhanwar Singh as an escort to the stretcher parties being used to ferry the wounded. Returning alone from one such excursion, Bhanwar Singh was midway between Kodda and Barisal when three Pakistani Razakars jumped at him; the trio had an LMG and three rifles.

Bhanwar knew he did not have too many options. He would either die right there, or it would be a slow lingering death as a Pakistani prisoner. With a ferocious cry, he boldly charged the enemy. So taken aback were the trio that they surrendered. Bhanwar Singh returned triumphantly to the battalion HQ with his three prisoners.

Tension remained high in Alpha Company in anticipation of a second strike. However, luckily the Pakistanis failed to press home their advantage.

Perhaps they too were caught up in the fog of battle and their commanders did not read the situation properly. Or perhaps they noted the arrival of reinforcements as Delta Company rushed in and co-deployed with Alpha. However, they certainly kept up the pressure on the guardsmen with small arms, artillery and tank fire.

The Akhaura strongpoint was heavily fortified and well stocked. Well enough to enable the Pakistanis to wage war for weeks. And the Indians did not have much time. Everyone was aware that it would not be long before the community of nations intervened and forced the guns to go silent. The Americans and the Chinese had already started raising the issue in several forums. It was possibly Russia's stand that held them at bay. But it was evident that it would not last for too long.

Charlie Company commanded by Tuffy Marwah, moving with the battalion HQ, found its way to the designated objective, Barisal, with relative ease. That is to say if one discounts the tedious, night-long trek through mud and slush, and, of course, the enemy guns that kept them engaged and amused through the night.

Within minutes of the fog lifting, the Pakistani artillery and armour ensured Charlie Company had to dig in and keep their heads down.

Realizing that most of the artillery fire that was making life difficult for his men was coming from one particular gun position, Himmeth tasked Tuffy to raid the gun position.

Fortunately, or unfortunately, depending on the point of view one takes, by the time Tuffy's raiding party hit the gun position, the Pakistanis had pulled back their guns to an alternate position.

Meanwhile, back at the battalion HQ, another drama was unfolding. Naik Jai Singh, who was serving with the unit's Intelligence Section, learnt that Subedar Rawat, the senior JCO of

Bravo Company, had been wounded. He, however, could not be evacuated due to heavy enemy fire.

Honorary Captain Jai Singh

'Subedar Rawat was also from Alwar, my hometown,' said Jai Singh, who eventually retired as an Honorary Captain. 'I had already lost one of the boys from my village the previous day, and wasn't going to allow something to happen to Rawat. So I told Commandant sahib that I was going to Bravo Company to bring him back.'

It was only when night fell that Himmeth finally relented and allowed an obstinate Jai Singh to go. Under cover of darkness, Jai Singh, with another guardsman, stealthily made his way into Bravo Company location. Braving their way through intense fire, the duo finally arrived.

'I found Subedar Rawat lying under a wooden bed in a tin hut,' Jai Singh narrated. 'He was very badly injured but tried to shoot me with his sten gun when I crept into the darkened hut. Luckily, I called out to him in time and recognizing my voice, he did not fire.'

To get his bearings, Jai Singh lit a match. That immediately drew the wounded JCO's ire. Rawat shouted at him to put out the light, warning him that any light would immediately draw fire since the Pakistani gunners were dominating every inch of the Bravo Company position.

Examining his wounds, Jai Singh realized he was injured far more seriously that he had assumed, and needed to be evacuated immediately. Giving him a shot of morphine, Jai Singh first bandaged his wounds with field dressings. Then he even gave him a cup of black tea, since all the sugar and condensed milk they had carried had already been spoilt by the mud and slush. Finally, sedated by the morphine and now a lot more comfortable, Jai Singh took Subedar Rawat on his shoulder and carried him back to the battalion headquarters; which was three kilometres away, and almost every bit of it was blanketed by enemy fire.

Himmeth saw Jai Singh coming in with the wounded JCO, who was immediately treated by the doctor and then evacuated back to the ADS.

'Commandant sahib was very happy with me,' the now wizened Jai Singh said simply. 'But more than anything, I was thrilled that Subedar Rawat made it through the war. After retirement, we would meet very often, and he would tell his family how I had carried him back.'

I did not notice any pride in the man before me. But seeing him and hearing his story, it was not hard for me to understand how tough it would have been for the Pakistanis to hold on their own against men such as him.

Now Akhaura had been encircled and the guardsmen had to hold on till such time as the remaining two units of the brigade completed the task of capturing it and flushing the enemy out of it.

However, the enemy did not seem in the mood to cooperate. Also, if the Pakistanis wanted to get out of Akhaura alive, they definitely needed to get rid of the guardsmen blocking their rear. That's why, like cornered cats, for the next sixty hours, they inflicted hell on 4 Guards, especially those of Alpha Company who were in the forefront and thus took the brunt of the enemy response.

The night of 2nd December passed with repeated probes and jitter parties being sent out by the Pakistanis. Their armour, too, kept probing the guardsmen.

However, 4 Guards managed to hold them at bay with small arms fire and also the supporting artillery, which was by now firmly in action. Also supporting them was the battalion's mortar platoon, commanded most commendably by Captain RAK Maneck of 1 Sikh Light Infantry.

The dashing, rakish Maneck had arrived in 4 Guards earlier in the year; a disciplinary case. He was attached with 4 Guards for an enquiry whilst the unit was in the Mizo Hills. Just before war broke out, when 4 Guards got orders to move, they were also instructed to send Maneck to the HQ of an adjoining brigade. However, Himmeth requested Mishra to retain him, not just because they had taken a liking to him, but also because he happened to be mortar qualified, something which no other 4 Guards officer at that time was.

Captain RAK' Maneck

Lieutenant Colonel RAK' Maneck (Retd.)

Himmeth's decision to retain Maneck was to prove wise since he commanded the mortar platoon with great courage and distinction.

Hailing from this illustrious regiment myself, I had heard a lot about him and was looking forward to meeting Maneck. He proved to be every inch the diamond that the stories about him made him out to be. The passage of years had done nothing to dim the fire in his belly, or the mischief in his eyes.

The mortar platoon, deployed at Barisal, provided effective and accurate fire throughout the battle for Akhaura, despite losing a lot of its ammunition when the civilian porters panicked and ran.

Maneck was deployed so close to the action that he was actually able to see the attacking Pakistanis; and that is why the mortar fire was incredibly accurate.

'I remember him very well even now. Maneck sahib was something else,' the burly, bespectacled, gruff looking Honorary Captain Sube Singh still showed vestiges of the sportsman he had been in his younger days. 'He had an amazingly positive attitude… nothing seemed to faze him at all.'

Moving just behind the battalion HQ, the mortar platoon was barely thirty minutes out from Litchi Bagan (the firm base from which the guardsmen had been launched) when Pakistani artillery started up.

'Within minutes, the Mukti Bahini boys who had been helping us to carry our ammunition had vanished. We lost a lot of ammunition because of them,' Sube sounded irritated. 'When we left Litchi Bagan, all the clerks, barbers and everyone else had been given two rounds each to carry. This was the only lot that finally reached us because they stuck with us through everything. But most of the ammunition being carried by the Mukti Bahini and even our own rifle companies did not. The Bahini boys took off and our rifle companies were scattered around and almost constantly in contact with the enemy, so they could not get it to us,' Sube Singh paused momentarily to gather his thoughts. He appeared conscious of the tape recorder running in front of him and was perhaps anxious to get the facts right.

'As for our men,' he smiled wickedly, 'the same buggers whom I had to hound and cajole to dig their foxholes properly during training, now burrowed in like over-caffeinated rabbits soon as the shelling started.' He gave us another smile, as beatific as the previous one. 'And when the artillery shelling would stop, we had to pull them out and yell at them to get them moving again.'

However, when it was all calm after the very first round of shelling, all efforts to arouse Signal Operator Biswanath failed. He had gotten unlucky. The shell had landed close to him.

'It was so hard to believe. He didn't look dead,' Sube looked momentarily befuddled. 'And he had been alive just a few moments ago.'

Aware that the radio set and the drum of telephone wire Biswanath had been carrying was critical for the mortar platoon to provide fire support to the rifle companies, Sube Singh retrieved both from his body.

'The drum was very heavy and an awkward load to carry, but I lugged it along till the going became almost impossible due to the slush. Finally, when I just could not cope any more, I had to abandon it. But I still kept carrying the radio set.'

Then the mind numbing shelling started again. But they kept going.

When the two groups of men ran into each other, neither realized the enemy was in their midst.

'It was only when one of our boys in front began to shout that we realized they were Pakistani soldiers,' Sube Singh grinned. I guess the memory was as funny now as the reality had been shocking then. 'At first, no one reacted. We were all stunned. Then my boys forgot about the mortars we were carrying and tried to engage the Pakistanis, but it was all happening too fast and there was simply too much confusion around. The Pakistanis began to run away with my boys in chase.'

Regaining control of the platoon, they resumed the infiltration, moving just ahead of the battalion HQ.

The mortar platoon had barely crossed Akhaura when they got orders to deploy. Despite there being no cover available, Maneck deployed the platoon and brought the mortars into action.

By now the boys had gotten over the shock of shelling, and their morale was high. Three of the four rifle companies were in contact and the need for covering fire was critical. Requests flowed in simultaneously from both Alpha and Bravo companies ensuring the mortar platoon had no time to think. Just re-lay the mortars, check the settings and shoot. Soon the barrels were steaming hot.

'Maneck sahib used to check the fire orders I was preparing and I used to double-check the ones he made. We wanted to ensure we got every thing right.' Sube suddenly stopped and gave me an aggrieved look. 'You know what I remember very clearly of the war?' It was obviously a rhetorical question. 'In all those days, we must have provided fire support dozens of times to every company, but it was only Major Marwah who ever called back to say that he appreciated our efforts and that we had done a great job.'

Perhaps it was a long buried feeling that had been unleashed as he relived those moments.

'I remember that very clearly,' Sube Singh repeated, and then shrugged. 'Not that we did not do our best for the others also. But Marwah sahib was the only one who expressed his appreciation.'

Sube Singh waited for me to say something. I figured a response was required; the emotion did need to be acknowledged and put to rest. 'I quite understand, sahib. Life is like that; more so war. We tend to take our own for granted,' I gave my most supportive look. It seemed to pacify him, and he resumed.

'And the other thing I remember very clearly was that unlike in exercises, where we are always deployed in such a manner that one or the other of the rifle companies is able to give us protection, it was not the case during this operation. Though battalion HQ was not too far behind us, since they were deployed near a mosque, but they were not close enough to help us if were attacked. Almost throughout the war, we were pretty much on our own.' Sube Singh's passion shone through even today. It was easy to see the spirit that had driven the guardsmen forward that day.

'But nothing held us back. We gave our best, whenever and wherever we were asked to give fire support. The boys were just too good. And Maneck sahib… no matter what happened, he sustained us. I rarely saw him sleep, and he was always cheerful. He was always going around, talking to the men and keeping their spirits high,' Sube did not bother to hide his admiration.

Despite his best efforts, Maneck knew that Himmeth was not at ease. It was the coming dawn that bothered Himmeth, for with it would come the Pakistani armour. By now there could be little doubt in the minds of the Pakistani commanders about the Indian intent and force levels; it was certain that they would do their utmost to stall the offensive and dislodge them. Time and terrain both stood firmly in favour of Pakistan.

Knowing that his boys would not be able to withstand the Pakistani armour without anti-tank weapons, Himmeth sent Captain Sahni back to get the RCL guns up post haste.

As the second bloody day drew to a close, Sahni headed back to look for the missing RCL guns. To do that, he had to find their tanks; which were supposed to have delivered the RCL guns to them.

'We had initially harboured at the old Malanchabas Palace Grounds, behind the Governor's house,' Lieutenant Raj Mohan pointed out. 'Later my troop was shifted to Litchi Bagan where 4 Guards were located.'

'Is that when you first met the unit?' I had a hazy idea of the cavalryman before me, or his role in those sixteen bloody days.

'No, no. I first came in contact with 4 Guards early in 1971,' the lanky cavalryman was smiling as he embraked down memory lane. 'I had been sent to collect our fourteen tanks, which were arriving by a special military train at Dharamnagar, the last rail-head in Tripura. I then had to take these tanks down an old, partly metalled road, which had many small bridges and culverts.'

Many of these bridges and culverts were so small that they would have collapsed with the weight of a tank. That necessitated leaving the road and navigating dozens of slushy rivers and nullahs. To make matters more interesting, Raj was only allowed to travel in hours of darkness, to keep the presence and number of tanks a secret from the Pakistanis.

'The atmosphere was already surcharged with war clouds,' Raj explained. 'On both sides, troops had begun to muster and hectic preparations were underway. In fact, sporadic clashes and exchange of fire, even artillery fire, had become quite the norm.'

Raj and his caravan of fourteen tanks seemed to have been on the road forever before they arrived. It was late evening when the first tank reached the Teliamura hilltop. It was the same hill that would later on become the tactical HQ of 4 Corps of the Indian Army, which, under Lieutenant General Sagat Singh, would lead the dash to Dacca.

'I can never forget that sight. The whole skyline was orange and the countryside seemed to roll away from me endlessly,' Raj breathed in awe. 'It was one of those nights when both sides were engaged in yet another artillery duel. The deep rolling boom of artillery guns filled the air. I could actually see flashes of light in the distance as the shells landed,' he tapped his forehead with a rigid forefinger. 'I can see it so clearly even now.'

So vividly had he described it that, so could I.

'Is that where you met 4 Guards?'

'No. That happened a bit later. When I was ordered to move from Malanchabas Palace Grounds to the Litchi Bagan-Shal Bagan area, that is where they were also located,' added Raj.

The Commandant Lieutenant Colonel Himmeth Singh was the first officer Raj encountered when he drove into the 4 Guards location.

'Himmeth was Himmeth,' Raj smiled at the memory. 'And there can never be another like him. The guy was unique. He and that Sikh Light Infantry officer who was attached as their mortar officer, Captain Maneck. I can never forget the two of them,' he added.

The young cavalry Lieutenant had been with 4 Guards for some time and must have made a fabulous impression on Himmeth. Towards the end of November 1971, just as they stood poised on the brink of war, Raj was ordered by his Squadron Commander Major Shamsher Mehta (who eventually retired as a Lieutnant General) to report to HQ 59 Brigade at Kailasher, bordering Sylhet, about fifty kilometres away, where he was to operate as part of an adhoc squadron.

Major Shamsher Singh Mehta (Shammi) 63 Cavalry

Lieutenant General Shamsher Singh Mehta, PVSM, AVSM & Bar, VSM (Retd.)

Himmeth came to know about Raj's departure just after the youngster had driven away. By then he had become so used to having him around and impressed by him that Himmeth refused to contemplate going to war without him. And he communicated the same to Major Shamsher Mehta, apparently with enough conviction to have him do something about it. Shamsher Mehta by now knew Himmeth well enough to know that once he made up his mind, it was hard to convince him otherwise. Mehta did not even try.

'I reached Kailasher at about 0200 hours and was walking out to stretch my legs after reporting to the Brigade Major (BM), Major Pandit, also a cavalry officer, when this huge, tall NCO from 4 Guards came up to me and told me that Colonel Himmeth and Major Mehta wanted him back immediately.' Raj elaborated.

As is the norm in armies across the world, the order was phrased as a request, but delivered as an order. Raj took note of the stress laid by the guardsman on the last word, now. Without another word, he headed back to the BM and informed him that he was returning to Litchi Bagan.

The BM suggested that instead of driving back again the whole night, Raj could catch the early morning Kailasher-Khowai-Agartala flight operated by Indian Airlines, if he moved fast, considering it was early morning already.

Grabbing his bags, Raj rushed. When he drove up to the airport, he could see the Indian Airlines Avro aircraft taxi-ing down the runaway. The cavalryman raced his one-tonner vehicle down the runaway, catching up and hurtling parallel to the aircraft, trying to catch the pilot's eye. That obviously did not take much effort, since one-tonner Army vehicles racing with aircrafts is not something one encounters often!

'The pilot actually stopped the aircraft and when I explained the urgency of my situation, he was sweet enough to take me on board, that too without a ticket,' explained Raj.

I could easily see the resource and intiative that Himmeth must have seen in him back then.

'When I got off the aircraft, the first person I saw was Himmeth. He was getting out of a MI4 helicopter,' he said. There were a couple of other officers with him. They had just returned from an aerial recon, during which they had been fired upon several times and quite effectively, as was evident from the number of bullet holes that Raj spotted strewn across the chopper.

'The unit was in uproar when I got back. Orders had been received and last minute preparations were in full swing,' said Raj.

Now that it was certain the unit would be going to war very soon, the next evening Himmeth threw a lavish dinner party.'Can you imagine?' Raj gave one of those looks. 'We were right in the front line, barely five clicks from the border. There was hell breaking loose all around us and Himmeth was giving dinner parties. And not just any odd party,' Raj waved grandiously. 'It was better than any five-star dinner I have ever attended,' he added, laughing. 'Even the Pakistanis must have been surprised to hear the 4 Guards bagpipers, since each one of us was piped into the mess, as per their battalion's tradition.'

And it did not just end there. The next morning, Himmeth even took Mehta for a farewell round of golf. One for the road, as it were!

'A few hours later, we went to war,' Raj paused, as though now surprised by the sudden contrast. 'Almost immediately, we ran into miles and miles of slush and marsh.'

Another half hour later, Raj and his tanks were being hammered by Pakistani artillery fire.

Before long, they had sailed into the hailstorm of bombs and bullets that had engulfed Akhaura. And all that stood between him and the enemy was a flimsy piece of pagri tied around his waist, masking the gap hole in the seat of his trousers.

The fourteen PT 76 tanks that could have proved invaluable in keeping the Pakistanis at bay were firmly stuck in the slush. A curtain of darkness kept them safe. But come morning, they would be sitting ducks for the Pakistani Air Force, the tanks and the two RCL guns of 4 Guards, which Himmeth so desperately needed upfront, with his rifle companies.

DAY THREE

03 DECEMBER 1971

'Both our RCL guns were still stuck at the *nullah* with the tanks when Captain Sahni found us. He told us what was happening up ahead, and how desperately we needed to get the RCL guns up to the rifle companies. He ordered us to get one detachment ready to move forward with 18 Rajput and join the battalion. We all knew how tough it was going to be to man-pack the RCL, but there was no choice; our boys needed us to hold the Pakistani tanks at bay.'

Mukund said this simply, without any embellishments. However, I could well imagine the mammoth task they had undertaken. I did not have to close my eyes to visualize them getting the guns off the tanks and carrying them through the slush. Dragging them through it would have been impossible, so they would have to be physically carried; no mean task considering the barrel alone weighs one hundred and fourteen kilograms and the gun mount another ninety-seven kilograms. Mukund must have been doing some mind reading since his next words vocalized what I was thinking.

'We knew we would not be able to carry the gun through the slush so we cut some bamboos and made stretchers to man-pack the gun, the mount and the ammunition on three separate stretchers,' he said.

I have handled the RCL during my days in uniform, and knew even that would have not made the task much easier.

How much worse had the Pakistani artillery and Air Force pounding at them made it? I could only imagine. For a moment my mind wandered away, gripped by a random thought—what is it about war and adversity that brings out such determination and resilience in men?

Mukund's voice pulled me out of my thoughts as he resumed the narrative.

'Somehow we managed to get that RCL across the railway line along which Bravo Company was deployed. The Rajputs crossed from the left of Bravo and we were right behind them. I would never have imagined it could get worse, but it did. The mud and slush across the railway line was terrible; neck deep at times. Despite all our precautions the barrel slipped and landed in the mud. Everything was so slippery that we were unable to get it out of the slush. That is when I hurt my back, while we were trying to pick up the barrel again.' Returning to the present he gave me a long look: 'It hurts even now.'

There was nothing for me to say. I didn't. He continued.

'You know, every time I think about that day, all I can remember is that there was no clear thought in my head. It was as though we were swimming through a sea of uncertainty and confusion, and lots of slush!'

I have been in battle. I knew that feeling. Perhaps that is why I had to ask: 'So tell me, what kept you guys going forward?'

'Only the knowledge that our boys needed us to get the RCL guns up. Otherwise they would have been totally at the mercy of the Pakistani tanks. We all knew they were banking on us to get there as fast as possible. So we somehow got the barrel out of the mud and then washed it clean in the river. Then about five hundred metres from the railway line, we hit a small bamboo cluster and halted there. By now, most of us had even run out of drinking water. The funny thing was that despite the cold, we were sweating like crazy. And, of course, by now all of us were totally covered in mud. I was so desperate for a drink of water that I finally requested one of the Rajput NCOs passing by for a drink. He gave me his water bottle. One sip and I almost gagged. It was filled with rum!'

All of us in the room joined in when he laughed.

'You don't drink?' I asked.

'I used to, but not so much, and in any case rum hardly quenches your thirst. When you need water, you need water!' Mukund gave me that when-you-gotta-go-you gotta-go look and a sheepish smile.

'Captain Saini told me that the *paltan* was close by, so we should get in touch right away. We established radio contact with the *paltan* and then leaving the gun in the bamboo grove with some of the boys, we went forward to link up. It was very tough finding anyone since enemy artillery was continuously going hammer and tongs at us. Finally, we spotted Lieutenant K.S. Yadav, the IO.'

Yadav must have noticed that the RCL detachment were at the end of their tether. He ordered some men from the admin group to carry the guns ahead and they finally reached the battalion HQ on the morning of 03 December 1971. Himmeth immediately ordered them to take up position in Alpha Company location since he knew they were the ones under maximum pressure.

Unknown to the guardsmen embroiled in battle with the Pakistanis at Akhaura, strange events had started unfolding in Jaipur.

'We only learnt much later,' Tuffy explained, 'that the Pakistanis had recovered our operational orders and the artillery fire plan from the body of MP Singh's radio operator.'

A little later, Pakistani radio announced that 4 Guards had been decimated and many of them also captured. No one could really confirm how this news mutated, but picking up on it, BBC shortly announced that Himmeth had been killed during this operation.

Several people the world over heard the BBC telecast. Amongst them were Major Durga Das and Colonel Govind Singh, both retired Armoured Corps officers living in Jaipur, which was also where Himmeth's home was.

Shocked, both officers went to Himmeth's house to pay their respects and offer their condolences. They were even more shocked when they found Himmeth's wife happily spending family time with his brother and sister-in-law. Not sure what to make of it, both of them left after a while without saying a word to her about Himmeth's demise.

'It was only much later, when it became clear that Himmeth was still alive,' Paunchy said with a laugh, 'that they mentioned this to Himmeth's wife. They told her that when they'd seen her so happy and cheerful, they did not have the heart to break the horrid news to her.'

Meanwhile, back on the battlefield, the RCL detachment had yet to reach Kodda when, on 03 December, at about 1100 hours, the Pakistanis launched a full-scale attack, with two companies drawn from 33 Baluch, 12 Azad Kashmir (AK) and 12 Frontier Force. The enemy attacked with full *josh*, and no matter how the battle ended, one cannot go on without a mention of the valour shown by the Pakistani soldiers.

The Pakistani Battalion Commander chose to launch two companies in a full frontal assault in broad daylight. Perhaps he had believed that Alpha Company would be jittered out of position just by seeing the mass effect of this Greek type of formation. However, when that did not happen, he decided to go ahead with the attack.

'We were lucky the Pakistanis did not use the north-south axis for their attack, although there was a clear gap they could have exploited,' Paunchy explained. 'They did not do that for the strangest possible reason. You see, earlier that morning, the Pakistanis sent a cow into the gap between the water tanks, the one where we had planted the few mines. They must have wanted to probe the gap for landmines.'

The cow did no damage. However, the Pakistanis did not relent. They now sent in a local, a Bengali villager.

The Alpha Company men saw the villager approaching the mined area and tried to scare him away by shouting at him. However, that did not deter him; he must obviously have been ordered by the Pakistani soldiers not to stop, and would have been mindful of their guns trained on him.

'I even took a shot at him to scare him away,' Paunchy did not look very happy about that. 'It was at a very extreme range for a carbine, but I think I grazed him by mistake because he shouted and clutched his wrist.'

Just then the cow stumbled back into the gap and stepped on one of the M-14 mines. The mine leaped out and exploded with a roar and a dirty black cloud. It killed both the cow and the hapless Bengali who'd been pushed forward by the Pakistanis.

That must have convinced the Pakistanis that the Indians had mined this gap, and they decided to stay away from it.

'They could not have known that we had barely used five or six mines,' Paunchy grinned, 'luckily for us, because an attack along that axis would have split our defences and we would have been in trouble.'

Due to this, the Pakistani attack came across open paddy fields and was subject to brutally effective enfilade fire from the Indian machine guns. Also, having utilized the night gainfully, by now Alpha Company was dug in and much more firmly deployed. Seeing the attack developing, Paunchy now called for artillery and mortar support.

By now, all the artillery resources available to the brigade had been pooled in and made available to Mahipal Singh to support Alpha Company. Though under constant enemy fire, and unmindful of his personal safety, Singh used them skillfully. He wreaked havoc on the Pakistani attackers.

'We kept calling for artillery fire even when the Pakistanis were as close as thirty metres to our trenches,' Paunchy clarified. 'Mahipal had warned me that we were too close, and friendly fire could cause our own causalties, but the attack was so massive that my choices were limited.'

As it turned out, both Paunchy and Mahipal were right. The Indian 5.5 inch medium battery shells did help break up the Pakistani assault. And they did cause a couple of Indian casualties also. One of the unfortunates was Lieutnant Karmakar, the Alpha Company officer.

2nd Lieutenant
S. M. Karmarkar

Major S.M. Karmarkar
(Retd.)

'Even today, the poor guy lives with about twenty shell splinters in his back,' Paunchy shook his head ruefully.

Tuffy Marwah saw the Pakistanis begin to gather in the west. He did the math and knew an attack on Alpha Company was imminent. He saw the enemy's fire support group move into position.

Tuffy immediately realized that if he could move a team about five hundred metres forward, he would be able to make life very difficult for the Pakistani fire support group. Up ahead in the distance, he could even spot the ideal position from which he would be able to bring deadly effective, enfilade fire on them. The problem was that between him and that position was five hundred metres of flat, open ground. There wasn't an iota of cover available anywhere. Tuffy knew that he could well be signing the death warrant of whomsoever he sent out for this job. It took him only a moment to decide. Warning Paunchy and Himmeth, he moved.

Marshalling three LMGs from the nearest platoon, Tuffy headed for the firing position he had chosen. The Pakistanis spotted him immediately. Within seconds, a hailstorm of bullets and bombs was headed his way.

Perhaps fortune does favour the brave. It seemed as though there was a protective bubble around Tuffy and his band of machine gunners. Barring a few scrapes, bumps and the odd splinter injury, they reached their objective unscathed.

Now it was the turn of the Pakistani fire support group to suffer. Right through the Pakistani attack on Alpha Company, Tuffy forced their fire support group to keep their heads down, reducing their effectiveness to near negligible levels.

Tuffy was still there when the Pakistani attack faltered, broke, and they began to fall back in shambles. Many more fell to his waiting guns.

It is certain that every Pakistani soldier who took part would have known the sheer folly of such an assault, yet not one of them faltered. The result was a foregone conclusion, yet one has to salute such bravery, even in the enemy. The attack was as ill-conceived as the charge of the Light Brigade. The result was certainly as unfortunate—33 Baluch lost seventy-five men and 12 AK had thirty killed, including an officer. So intense and accurate was the Indian firing that the Pakistanis, in their hurry to get away, left sixty-six of their bodies behind.

'That was the exact number,' Paunchy said with conviction, 'because when I went back to Kodda last year, I actually spoke to one of the villagers who had been there at that time.

He remembered they had buried sixty-six Pakistani bodies. I have it on videotape.'

With the back of the attack broken, the Pakistani troops began to fall back in disarray.

By now, the guardsmen of Alpha Company were running low on ammunition. Realizing this, the Company Senior JCO Subedar Makhan decided to innovate a bit. A Jat from Haryana, Makhan was a World War II veteran and had also seen intense action in Kashmir. He was a solid, unflappable man, fast on his feet and seldom perturbed by anything, no matter how fraught the situation.

Ordering his boys to use the 303 rifles they had captured earlier that morning from the Pakistani Razakars, Alpha Company began to pick off the fleeing enemy.

So intense was the carnage that several Pakistani soldiers hit the ground and played dead. Unfortunately, a smoke grenade being carried by one of the Pakistani soldiers exploded and set fire to the dry paddy that had been harvested only recently. The fire stampeded those who had been pretending to play dead and they got up to run. None of them got very far.

The Pakistani companies that had been decimated during this brave, but ill-conceived attack had constituted the 14 Pak Infantry Divison reserves. Their loss seriously unsettled the Pakistanis. So much so that they now called for an air strike.

Moments later, four F-86 Sabre jets screamed in. They carried out three rocketing and strafing runs over the target area. Luckily for the guardsmen, they were so close to the Pakistani frontline that the Sabres left them alone. However, 18 Rajputs, a little further away, took the brunt of this airstrike. Luckily, they suffered no major damage.

As soon as the attack broke, Paunchy moved forward with a section to mop up and ensure there was no enemy still lingering in the area. They were sweeping over the company front when something on the wrist of one of the dead Pakistani soldiers caught his eye. It looked familiar. Paunchy went closer. It was.

Paunchy retrieved the HMT wristwatch that he had not so long ago gifted to his batman, Lance Naik Pirbhu Ram.

Perhaps this was God's way of delivering punishment on the now dead Pakistani, a soldier from 33 Baluch: all professional soldiers frown upon looting and pilfering: it is not the warrior's way.

Paunchy tucked the HMT watch in his pocket, and resolved to deliver it to Pirabhu's family. He knew they would cherish it as much as Pirabhu had.

Seeing the Pakistani attack building up against Alpha Company, Captain Maneck brought the battalion 81 mm Mortars into action immediately. Directed by the Mortar OP with Alpha Company, the mortars began to rain fire on the Pakistanis as they gathered for the assault. The mortar platoon was deployed near Chandi, and Maneck could actually eyeball the incoming assault; perhaps that is why his mortar fire had such deadly effect.

By now, however, the Pakistani artillery was also in action. Within minutes, the 4 Guards Mortar platoon drew their ire. The very first Pakistani artillery salvo scored, taking out the mortar on the extreme left.

'That is when we lost Uday Bhan,' Sube's gaze was fixed on something in the distance. He obviously found the memory upsetting even now. 'Uday Bhan was a rock solid guy. The boys were very upset when we lost him. But we kept going … there was no time to think.' He was silent for a little while, and when he did resume his tone, it had gone mellow. 'We kept firing almost nonstop, moving from one fire task to the other.'

Despite the intense counter-bombardment, egged on by Maneck, the remaining mortars continued providing defensive fire to Alpha Company. However, Alpha Company's problems were mounting. They increased further as, once again, a Pakistani tank came into view. Following closely behind it was some Pakistani infantry.

Seeing the tank bearing down on them, Paunchy thanked his stars that at least one of the RCL guns was with him now. Sahni had delivered it just moments ago.

'Major C.K. sahib was very happy to see us when we reached with our RCL,' said Mukund, with a smile that communicated relief, which must have been mutual: Paunchy's at finally getting an anti-tank weapon, and for Mukund's detachment, at the opportunity to be able to support their rifle companies after being stuck in the mud and blasted by enemy artillery and air for all these hours.

They had just finished deploying the RCL near the MMG detachment commanded by Naik Didar Singh when first light arrived. With it came another Pakistani assault, led by a tank, which came thundering up along the railway line.

'Didar was amazing. He took out several Pakistani soldiers before the tank began to lay down suppressive fire. The tank was using its machine gun, not the main gun, but its fire was very effective. Nothing happened to Didar, but one of the tank machine gun rounds smashed into the charging handle of my RCL's spotting rifle,' Mukund gave an exasperated cluck. 'It got jammed, and no matter what we tried, we could not free it.'

Captain Sahni, who had helped deliver the RCL gun to Alpha Company, saw them struggling with the charging handle. Realizing something was amiss, he made his way forward and tried to hammer the charging handle loose. Sahni was doing that when his knee accidentally hit the firing knob and the RCL main gun, which had just been loaded, fired.

'The RCL was already pointed in the general direction of the Pakistani tank,' Mukund's smile was full of mischief. 'It didn't hit the tank but must have spooked him enough to take off.'

After that, the enemy tanks did not venture near Alpha Company. In fact, things began to actually quieten down a bit.

'The artillery and mortars were still pounding at us, but by now we were also becoming somewhat used to them,' Mukund added after a moment's thought. 'I don't mean we were taking it lightly or anything because every now and then they would get lucky and someone would get injured. But…' he shrugged, 'you know how it is … how long can anyone stay hunkered down?'

Also, by now, hunger pangs had begun gnawing at the RCL gunners. The mud, slush and river water had ruined the food they had been man packing. Even water was running low. Mukund, of course, had run dry several hours ago.

So, braving the occasional artillery shell that lit up the sky sporadically, and the firefly-like pinpricks of machine guns, Mukund forayed for food. There were a couple of abandoned houses around, but the pickings were slim and Mukund returned empty-handed.

The RCL gunners slept on empty stomachs yet again. Not that they slept much; the constant rumble of guns ensured that.

And with the new dawn came new orders—for the RCL detachment to link up with Delta Company.

It had been a long night for Delta Company as well. By now casualties had mounted and, as with the rest of the unit, the food was ruined and there was very little water too.

Granthi had finished briefing Himmeth about the situation and was walking away when Captain Maninder called out to him.

'Don't let them send me back, sir,' Maninder had overheard the conversation between his Company Commander and the Commandant, and knew Granthi had been ordered to get the wounded and dead back. 'Please, I need to be with the boys. I will be fine. Really.'

'LM was crying… He was a very fine regimental officer,' Granthi suddenly broke off. Struggling, but not succeeding in holding back his tears.

We all looked away.

'Bravo Company had been pinned down for hours by now. Things were going from bad to worse really fast,' said Midha as he re-lived those moments. 'I could see the enemy loading and firing their 2-inch mortars at us. They were so close we could even hear them talking.'

The dead bodies had begun to accumulate. In addition to the dozen that had been wounded, another six, including Captain Sundaram, the Artillery OP, had given up their lives. So intense and accurate was the firing that the guardsmen could not even get out of the trenches. Consequently, by now, the stench of urine and excreta mingled with that of blood and gunpowder.

Unlike the others, one of the guardsmen could not countenance answering nature's call in his foxhole, and neither could he hold it out any longer. Steeling himself, he headed out of the foxhole.

'I couldn't see who it was, but he did not make it very far,' Midha gave a sad headshake. 'One of the artillery shells landed almost directly on him. There was little left…' his voice trailed away, into a long silence.

'There was nothing we could do about our clothes, which were totally covered in mud and slush,' Midha grimaced, 'but I just could not think of keeping my wet socks on even for a minute longer. So the minute there was a little lull in the firing, I took off my boots and socks, to dry them out.'

He continued: 'Just then a 2-inch mortar bomb landed with a dull crump, barely a few feet away. Shards of splinters sprayed all around. I took a couple of them in my hand and my arm. At first, the shock was so much that I did not even realize I had been hit, and then even when the pain began I was not sure how badly I was injured. So I made my way across to a building some distance away and took shelter, in the space under the stairs. Just then another 2" mortar bomb landed next to me again and this time I took some splinters in the sole of my foot.' He grimaced: 'That hurt a lot.'

'Then? Did they evacuate you?' I asked.

'Evacuate? Are you kidding? There was so much firing and the Pakistanis were literally in our faces. Trying to get anyone out from there would have meant certain death. Not that I was the only one… By now the body count was climbing rapidly. Luckily, my bones had not been shattered, so I was managing,' he answered.

Bandaging the wound with a field dressing, Midha got back into the trenches and the firefight resumed, with the odds heavily loaded against the guardsmen. Food had been ruined by the slush, and water had run out. Ammunition also had started running low, forcing them to use it as sparingly as possible. They had no way of knowing when replenishments would reach them. After all, now the Pakistani defences at Akhaura lay between them and India.

Just when they thought things could get no worse, a Pakistani tank came up along the railway line.

The very first round fired by the tank hit the tree just beside Midha.

'I was starting to feel like a bloody lightning conductor. First the mortars had been following me around and now the tank.'

The tree was split apart, right down the middle.

A few more rounds from the tank's main gun wracked Bravo Company, before the tank fell silent, unable to spot a worthy target. However, it remained there, just beside the railway line, barely two hundred metres away, keeping a hawk's eye on Bravo Company.

Located between Midha and Kharbanda was Guardsman Kalu with his trusted 3.5" RPG. Midha wanted to take a shot at the tank with it, but the more experienced Kharbanda held him back. He was aware that the minute the RPG fired, it and the men around it would be dead meat; the RPG may or may not have been able to take it out, but the tank was just too close to miss.

With not many other options available to them, Midha decided to call for artillery and mortar support. It may or may not do much damage to the tanks, but would definitely impose caution on the Pakistanis and force them to keep their heads down.

On the artillery front, things were far from rosy. The brigade artillery resources had been severely depleted.

'You see,' (now) General Mahipal Singh explained, 'in addition to Sundaram and Iqbal being killed, three of the Artillery OP officers with the brigade, (Captains Thomas and Verma, and Second Lieutenant Uttam) and three of the radio operators and Technical Assistants (Dhankar, Paleram and Rajpal Singh) had been wounded,' Singh paused. For a moment, his solemnity broke. 'In fact, the manner in which Uttam was wounded was stranger than fiction.'

Uttam had been advancing with 18 Rajput when the enemy guns opened up. Several light and medium machine guns began to engage the Rajputs. The only place Uttam could find to take shelter was behind a telegraph pole. He was standing flush behind it, his body sheltered by it. However, that day the bullet with his number on it had been deployed. And not just one, but two of them. The first clipped his left ear off, and the second took away his right one.

'It may sound hilarious now, but then it was totally tragic,' Glucose explained. 'By now our artillery resources were so thin on the ground that we had to immediately move our Artillery OPs, Captain Nair and Lieutenant M.P. Singh to join the rifle companies up ahead and support them.'

By now a lot of the load had also fallen on the battalion's mortar platoon.

The 4 Guards mortar platoon had been in non-stop action since the first day. Ammunition would have been critically low if it had not been for the valiant efforts of Chauhan, Sahni and the so-called fundis, (administrative personnel) as well as some of the more valiant Mukti Bahini chaps who stuck it out through the shelling and enemy fire.

'Thankfully, ammunition kept coming in, but in all the confusion no one remembered to get food for us. It was only on the fourth day that the first consignment reached us; sixteen puris and seven oranges,' said Sube with amazing clarity.

Forty years had gone by since, and I could not resist reconfirming: 'You remember the exact number?'

'How could I not?' Sube laughed. 'There were twenty-seven of us in the mortar platoon that day and some Mukti Bahini boys.'

'So what did you guys do?' I was intrigued.

'Everyone was starving by now, so we just shared whatever there was and everyone got about one bite.' Then he added hastily, 'Not that I am complaining. We all understood that the rifle company boys in front were priority and needed to be fed and watered first. We were also under fire, but I am sure their plight was much worse since they were right in the enemy's face.'

It was Himmeth who first realized the plight of the mortar platoon and ensured they received food. But that happened only on the next day.

In that moment, the bloodbath was continuing.

DAY FOUR

04 DECEMBER 1971

When Himmeth walked into the Alpha Company location, Paunchy was nowhere to be seen. He learnt from Guardsman Ved Prakash, who was performing the duties of Paunchy's radio operator, that he had gone to answer nature's call. Sure enough, Paunchy returned a few minutes later, looking suitably relieved. Before Himmeth could say a word, Paunchy remarked, 'These Pakistanis have noses like dogs.'

Obviously he received a puzzled look from his Commandant.

'I have changed the timing so often, but it makes no difference. No matter what time I decide to go, they start shelling,' Paunchy explained. 'Buggers always manage to catch me with my pants down.'

Relieved to find his company commanders in such fine fettle, with their sense of humour intact despite the mayhem all around, Himmeth finished his round of the battlefield and headed back to the battalion HQ. He hoped the other companies were doing equally well and holding on their own.

From the face of it, Himmeth noted with satisfaction, despite their woes, they seemed to have the Pakistanis on the run.

Despite being well stocked and nicely dug in, by now the Pakistanis were very jittery. Battle fog was clouding the real picture, but they could see Indian troops all around them. The pressure on Akhaura was intense and building up from all directions. 4 Guards going around them and cutting them off from their rear had hit their morale far harder than an actual assault on Akhaura may have; it hammered at their will to fight.

By the next day, 4th December, the defences had begun to crack as the Pakistani spirit crumpled. With their command and control in disarray and already under pressure from the hostility of the local population, the first signs of a Pakistani pullback became evident. But the fight was not yet over. Not by a long shot.

That became clear when Himmeth got a report that the Pakistanis were trying to outflank Bravo Company, which was pinned down right under their nose.

'I was holed up quite close to my company senior JCO when we got word that Pakistanis were trying to outflank us,' Midha recollected. 'The senior JCO had been badly wounded and was being tended to by his *sahayak* (helper). I will never forget what I heard him say to his *sahayak*: "Go out and kill some Pakistanis… As many as you can… And if you see that our position is about to be overrun, come back and kill me. I don't want to be captured alive by the bastards,"' Midha gave a firm nod. 'I was so inspired by his words that I called my own helper Lakshman and gave him the same orders.' Then an acute sadness crossed his face. 'Lakshman went out and was hit by a splinter minutes later; he lost an eye.'

The situation was decidedly grim as Bravo Company steeled itself to meet the coming onslaught.

Himmeth was already aware that Indian armour could not get across the railway line, which was so constructed that it was a natural anti-tank obstacle. However, Bravo Company could not be left out to dry. Getting on the radio set, he explained the situation to Shamsher Mehta, the armoured Squadron Commander.

'If you don't do something fast, we are going to lose that company.' With Himmeth's words ringing in his ears, Shamsher got his boys together, gunned his tank and headed straight for the railway line and the Pakistanis who were getting ready to tackle Bravo Company.

Himmeth later narrated to Colonel Pyarelal how the armoured squadron dashed in to retrieve the situation for Bravo Company: I saw Raj's tank hit the railway embankment like a steeple-chaser. It soared over the embankment and landed on the other side with a resounding crash. I was certain that everyone inside the tank must have been knocked unconscious. However, apparently, Raj's head was also amoured. Guns blazing, the Indian tanks pressed on, straight for the Pakistani infantry that was massing for the attack.

Seeing that the Indians had been able to get their tanks to the west of the railway line, the Pakistani infantry decided to call it a day. They pulled back. And thereafter contented themselves with inflicting artillery and machine gun fire on Bravo.

Though the grave danger of being overrun had been thwarted for the moment, at Shyamnagar, Bravo Company's plight still remained precarious. Still pinned down near the Akhaura Railway Station, on the western bank of Titas river, they maintained eyeball to eyeball contact with the Pakistani defences.

Himmeth had nothing in his kitty to make their plight better. This was already the fourth day that they had been fighting it out on their own. No one had yet been able to get across to their position. Not even the administrative parties with food, water and ammunition. Barring morale, everything else was running low, and even that would not hold out forever. Aware that Bravo Company could not be left to its own resources much longer, he decided to do the only thing he could—go down and give them moral support. He wanted them to know they were not alone.

'I panicked when the old man told me he was going to Bravo Company location,' said a visibly agitated Glucose. 'I mean, Bravo were trapped barely a hundred fifty metres from the railway station and they were under relentless fire. The old man would be at huge risk.'

'We all heard him shouting at the Commandant not to go to Bravo Company,' Sube Singh grinned. The mortar platoon was deployed within earshot of the battalion HQ and had a ringside view of the high drama.

'It may sound silly now, but you have to understand that the *paltan* did not even have a second in command and all the company commanders were pretty junior. After Himmeth, the seniormost officer, Paunchy had barely nine years of service. The others were still to get their feet wet. I was petrified about what would happen to the unit if something happened to Himmeth. Who would have taken command of the unit?' Glucose asked. 'That is why I was damn upset. I had every reason to be,' he added emphatically.

Himmeth, of course, was not the kind to listen. Unwilling to leave his boys alone when they were in trouble, around midnight, he left with the administrative party that was taking food forward to Bravo Company. Accompanying him were both his radio operators and a couple of escorts.

Now alone in the battalion HQ, the twenty-four-year-old Glucose began to seriously panic.

'I came to know that Himmeth was dropping in to look us up. By now, we had six dead and sixteen wounded. Major Kharbanda had told me to keep an eye on them,' Midha clearly had vivid memories of Himmeth's visit that night. 'I immediately sent some men to get stuff ready to receive the old man.'

Not surprisingly, it was one of the Mukti Bahini boys who sneaked into one of the huts on the outskirts of Akhaura and literally brought home the bacon … well, chicken in this case. It was not long before the said chicken found itself being cooked on a makeshift stove.

Despite the mayhem and carnage all around them, when Himmeth arrived, he found Bravo Company had prepared a delicious chicken dish for him. He was as touched by the gesture as he was impressed with Midha's resourcefulness.

'I will never forget the report Himmeth gave me after that episode. He wrote just one line in my Annual Confidential Report): "He will make a good regimental officer." Since that day, whenever I have felt myself floundering or in doubt, I remember that report,' Midha's sense of pride was as palpable as Sube Singh's passion had been.

By the time Himmeth finished going around the trenches and talking to the Bravo Company boys, it was almost early morning.

Perhaps the Pakistanis spotted the antennae of the radio sets accompanying Himmeth and realized a senior officer was within easy gun range. They started hammering Bravo Company with everything they had.

'The firing became so intense and was so accurate that we were not able to move an inch. The slightest movement invited an immediate response,' Midha said. 'And that machine gunner was still very much on the ball. He, and the Pakistani spotter directing the artillery fire, seemed to be tracking Himmeth with deadly accuracy.'

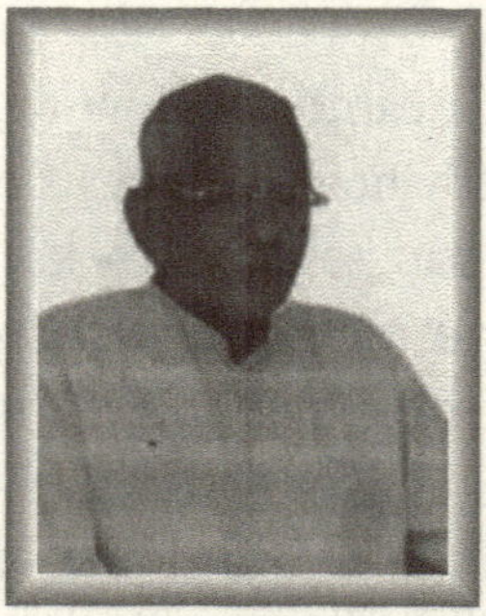

Guardsman Nahar Singh

There was not much cover available. Himmeth and Nahar Singh, the radio operator accompanying him, took cover in a tiny depression, more like a fold in the ground. It was so tiny that the two men could not fit it fully.

Realizing that his Commandant's hand was outside, in the open, Nahar Singh reached out and pulled it in. He had barely done so when an artillery shell landed nearby. One of the several flaming splinters that sprayed out tore away a part of Nahar Singh's hand.

'At that time, his hand was precisely where my hand had been just seconds ago,' Himmeth's recording to Pyarelal told me. It made me wonder what had gone through Himmeth's mind when he saw that. I wondered what would have gone through mine, had it been me back there. 'We bandaged his hand the best we could, but I could see the wound was major and he would need to be evacuated to a hospital else he would lose that hand.'

Nahar Singh refused to even consider being evacuated.

'It's a minor injury, sahib. Besides, I cannot go away. I have to man your radio set. And I want to be there with you when we enter Dacca,' was Nahar Singh's response.

Himmeth held his peace. Not that evacuation was even a possibility at that point. The enemy was still gunning for his party.

As light increased, so did the effectiveness of the Pakistani fire. Himmeth was pinned down with Bravo Company.

'I was literally in tears when I came to know that Himmeth was trapped with Bravo Company,' Glucose made no attempt to mask his feelings even now. 'I was on the verge of panic, knowing that if Himmeth was taken out, the unit was in serious trouble. As it is, we were behind enemy lines and under tremendous pressure from all sides.'

Desperate to extricate the Commandant, Glucose shrugged off emotions and focused on the task. He ordered the Forward Air Controller (FAC) to direct an airstrike at the Pakistani position opposite Bravo Company. He also ordered Maneck to lay down a smoke screen in front of Bravo defences.

The minute Maneck came to know about the situation, he re-directed all the mortars and they laid down barrage after barrage of smoke between Bravo and the enemy. For Maneck, it was not just a professional task. Where Himmeth was concerned, Maneck felt a deep emotional attachment, too.

'Despite being considered a trouble-maker, and against the advice of the top brass, Himmeth took me into the war with 4 Guards. He believed in me, trusted me… In fact, he often told me that I had not been handled well,' Maneck's admiration for the old man was abundantly visible. 'I was an Acting Captain but had been reduced to my substantive rank when I was attached to 4 Guards. Himmeth even spoke to the powers that be and got my acting rank restored when we went to war.'

Fired with this zeal, Maneck ensured his mortars landed with telling effect; to provide Himmeth the required screen to extricate.

Meanwhile, the air strike also arrived. It was deadly accurate and forced the Pakistani machine gun to go silent. However, the enemy artillery was already locked on to Bravo Company location and they continued with their deadly tattoo, affected neither by the air strike, nor by Maneck's mortars.

Willy-nilly, Himmeth managed to get back to the battalion HQ, bringing back the injured Nahar Singh with him.

One of the first things Himmeth did on reaching the battalion HQ was to have the doctor take a look at Nahar Singh's hand. Doctor Sutra confirmed what Himmeth had feared; the injury was a major one. Despite Nahar Singh's protests, Himmeth ensured Glucose put him on the first chopper out, back to the hospital.

Meanwhile the action all around 4 Guards was escalating rapidly.

At Kodda, Delta Company again attempted to capture the bigger bridge, which Alpha had tried on 2nd December.

'We were already in the Forming Up Place (FUP) when we realized the bridge had been reinforced by the Pakistani tank troops that had withdrawn from Akhaura. Now there was no way we could take that post with the resources available to us,' said

Granthi grimly. 'But by now we were hemmed in. The Pakistani artillery had ranged in and were really hammering at us. For a change, even our own artillery fire was a real pain since we were too close to the enemy, so friendly fire was hurting us as much as the enemy artillery.'

Just then, Lance Naik Dhuni Ram saw some Pakistani soldiers come running forward. They were trying to outflank his section. Knowing the section would be written off if that happened, Dhuni Ram stood up and boldly engaged them. He was wounded almost immediately, but kept firing and finally beat them up.

Not too far away from him, Lance Naik Chhotu Ram was also holding the Pakistanis at bay with his LMG. So effective was his fire that the enemy brought an RCL to bear on him. Chhotu was injured, yet he stuck to his guns and kept firing.

Despite the tremendous pressure they were under, Bravo continued to deny the enemy all movement along the riverbank and the Akhaura railway station. This proved to be of vital importance in enabling the capture of Akhaura by 18 Rajput on 05 December 1971. In addition, Bravo also inflicted a lot of losses on the Pakistanis during their withdrawal on 05 December. And they managed to capture intact the bridge across Titas river.

DAY FIVE

05 DECEMBER 1971

By now, the Forward Air Controller (FAC) Pilot Officer Daljit Singh Shaheed had reached Kodda.

Daljit, a youngster with barely one year's service, had joined 4 Guards as the FAC a few days before the war. He arrived armed with a puny little pistol, a big radio set and a bigger attitude: the kind that wins wars.

'Right from the first day, he hounded Himmeth to give him something to do,' Glucose grinned; for a moment giving a glimpse of why he had been so nicknamed. 'Something more active, I mean. Unable to resist his enthusiasm, Himmeth tasked him to look after the Prisoners of War (POWs) during the advance on Akhaura. Not content with that, Daljit insisted on being sent on patrols. The old man did send him out a couple of times, but refrained when he realized that he would be a hard man to replace in case of some unforeseen eventuality. And the chances of that were rather high because Daljit was one of those irreprehensible, boisterous characters. It was very hard to keep him in control. He was always up to something.'

Glucose thumped the arm of his chair. 'Let me tell you what he'd done just the previous day. A Pakistani machine gun bunker at Akhaura was continuously harassing us. Located along the line of the bund of the railway line that runs from Akhaura to Brahmanbaria, the bunker was a really tough target to take on. Daljit decided to take matters in hand and call in an airstrike, but we had no sorties available. Totally unfazed, he happily requisitioned a sortie that had actually been allocated for 73 Brigade. The requisition may have been dubious, but the strike was masterful, to say the least. Directed by Daljit, the strike leader flew in barely thirty feet off the ground. He hit the bunker with every rocket he fired. So did the other aircraft following in his wake.'

A long silence followed, as we all tried to imagine a modern, high-speed aircraft zooming on to a target at that height; thirty feet is barely treetop level.

By now the attack mounted on Akhuara by 18 Rajput and 10 Bihar had attained critical mass. It proved to be the last straw for the Pakistanis. Their nerves had already been rattled when 4 Guards had cut them off from behind. Now literally under siege from all sides, they just got up and started to run away.

The bridge on the Akhaura-Brahmanbaria railway track, which first, Alpha and then Delta Company of 4 Guards had tried to capture, fell to the Rajputs almost immediately. It broke the back of the Akhaura defences totally. The Pakistanis fled helter-skelter. Within minutes, the tone of the battle had altered dramatically.

'It became a duck shoot,' Paunchy cut in. 'They were running right across our front and our boys shot down many of them.'

The same scenario was also playing out in front of Bravo Company. The Pakistanis fleeing in panic fell to the guns of the waiting guardsmen.

'Most of them were from 33 Baluch, as we discovered from the dead bodies,' Glucose added. 'It was a total rout.'

The five PT 76 tanks that had made life miserable for Alpha Company the previous day also fell into the hands of the guardsmen. It was only now that Paunchy found out the real reason why they had refrained from attacking him, or from using their main guns on him. Due to non-availability of spares, the main guns of all five tanks were no longer functional.

Operation 'Nut Cracker', the investment and capture of Akhaura had succeeded.

Akhaura was a vital block on the road to Dacca, and its capture did crack the Pakistanis. Now the Indian forces had broken past the hard outer shell and were inside the soft kernel; which proved to be much softer than what the Pakistanis had imagined it to be.

Himmeth got the message that Brigadier Mishra was on his way forward. They decided to meet at Bravo Company location. Himmeth was soon back in the same location from where he had barely escaped alive just hours ago. However, now, the mood of the boys was remarkably different. Their morale was sky high and the guardsmen were raring to pick up the chase and hunt down the withdrawing Pakistanis.

As evening fell, the two commanders bent their heads over the map, in the light of a lantern, and began to confer. Unaware that, a few metres away, shielded by the fading light, a wounded Midha was listening to every word.

'Life seldom gives us such opportunities, sir,' Midha heard Himmeth tell the Brigade Commander. 'God knows when we will get the orders to advance… By then, it might be too late. I think we should just keep the pressure on and go after the enemy. This is a chance of a lifetime… We should not give them any time to stabilize.'

Both were obviously experienced commanders and unwilling to let this golden opportunity pass, since that is precisely what they did. Mishra told Himmeth to press on while the Pakistanis were still falling back in complete disarray.

The guns had barely fallen silent on Akhaura and the Pakistanis were still pulling back helter-skelter when 4 Guards resumed the chase.

'I cannot tell you how I felt when I heard them talking,' Midha was clearly emotional. 'It made my morale soar. Suddenly, all the death and destruction that we had lived through the past four days seemed to become worthwhile.'

Though raring to be part of the chase, the injured Midha was ordered to get the dead and wounded back to the ADS, which had been established on the IB.

As night fell, the cold deepened. Surrounded by the dead and wounded, Midha shivered through the freezing night. All around him, he could hear the battalion getting ready to advance.

Unaware of all this, Alpha Company was busy collecting the bodies of the seven men from Desraj's platoon, which they had been unable to do earlier.

'I don't know whether you know what happens to a body when it has been lying out in the open for a couple of days,' the expression on Paunchy's face was hard to describe, an admixture of pain and anger.

I didn't. Not sure of what to say, I just shook my head.

'The bodies were in pathetic condition; covered with ants, flies and blue-bottles … some even partially eaten by dogs.' He looked sick at the memory, as I did simply listening to him. 'We finally got them on stretchers and then Subedar Makhan delegated twenty-eight of my boys to take them back to the Quartermaster, a few kilometres to the rear.'

The stretcher party had been gone about half an hour when Himmeth gave the orders for the unit to commence advance to Arhand. Pursuant to the discussion between Mishra and Himmeth, the Brigade Commander had ordered him to resume advance and set-up a roadblock at Arhand. The plan was to dominate the Brahmanbaria-Chittagong highway, the main artery between the two Pakistani formations opposing them.

'The taste of victory had yet to seep in when we got orders from Brigade HQ to move ahead and establish a roadblock at Arhand by first light,' said Glucose. He quickly drew a rough sketch of it for me, as he realized that the civilian map was inadequate. 'Though there was no time for reconnaissance to be carried out, and we were battered and exhausted after five days of non-stop action, our morale was high and the boys were raring to go.'

But Alpha Company was in no condition to resume advance. They had already lost half of Desraj's platoon during the Pakistani counter-attack on the smaller bridge. Another twenty-eight men (almost a complete platoon) was ferrying the dead bodies back to the Quartermaster, Captain Pradhan, so that he could dispose them of properly. In fact, if the battalion had not received a large number of reservists just prior to commencement of operations, Alpha Company would no longer have had the manpower to exist as an independent entity.

By now Paunchy was getting worried; it had been quite a while since his men had been gone with the bodies and there was no sign of them. When he finally managed to get through to them on Pradhan's radio set, he learnt that they were being sent back to Agartala with the bodies for proper disposal since Pradhan had no resources available with him to conduct their last rites.

'I don't blame Pradhan, but there was no way I could allow that… I would have had no manpower left for anything. Already Himmeth was putting a lot of pressure on all of us to get going.' At his wit's end, Paunchy threw the ball at Himmeth, who, with no other options available to him, took the hard call; he ordered

Pradhan to muster up something and cremate the bodies wherever he was and send Paunchy's men back to him immediately.

That is why it was almost 2200 hours by the time the unit managed to get going. The casualties had been tended to, the serious ones sent back to the ADS (Advanced Dressing Station) at Agartala, ammunition had been replenished and redistributed, and food and water distributed. More than anything else, everyone's morale was at a new high.

'We were supposed to start out at 2000 hours. This two-hour delay would cost us dearly, as we learnt later,' Paunchy looked woebegone.

DAY SIX

06 December 1971

'We must have gone about an hour when we saw some men coming towards us,' Sube Singh said. 'At first we thought they were our own boys, but as they were crossing us, someone suddenly shouted that they were Pakistanis. Before I could realize what was happening, my men began to run after them.'

Realizing the importance of keeping the platoon intact and ready to deploy and provide fire support at short notice, Sube Singh ran around and got his men back into order. By then the mortar platoon had captured two of the fleeing Pakistani soldiers.

Passing on the prisoners of war back towards the rear, the mortar platoon resumed its advance towards Arhand, approximately six kilometres away.

Flying in the dark, literally, Tuffy, who was leading the battalion's advance, had been banking on his local guides to get him to Arhand. However, even they got confused, and missing Arhand, landed bang on National Highway No 1.

Finally figuring out where they were, Tuffy got them going again and managed to hit Arhand by about 0300 hours on 06 December 1971. As instructed, he halted about half a kilometre short of Arhand and deployed. Following hard on his heels, the rest of the *paltan* quickly built up on Tuffy's position.

Himmeth ordered Paunchy to move ahead and recce out suitable deployment positions for the companies and for the roadblock.

'I had gone ahead with my radio operator and two riflemen to check out deployments positions when we suddenly heard the sound of people moving and the rumble of vehicles. We made it off the road just in time,' said Paunchy. Crouching by the side of the road, Paunchy and his trio of men saw about forty or fifty Pakistanis marching down the road, moving away from Arhand.

'We were just off the road, so close,' Paunchy pointed towards a flowerpot at the end of the corridor, about ten metres away. 'And not just the men, a whole Pakistani artillery battery moved past and we could only watch helplessly. It was perhaps not scary, but decidedly hair-raising,' he chuckled at the memory. 'It also made us realize that had we moved out from Akhaura in time; the road block would have been in position by now and we could have captured the whole battery without any hassles,' he gave a rueful cluck. 'It was a pity. This same artillery battery would cause many casualties later.'

As soon as it was safe to move, Paunchy returned to the battalion HQ and briefed Himmeth on the lie of the land.

Arhand is a small grove on the Brahmanbaria-Comilla highway. On this road were two culverts. Paunchy chose the area between the culverts to set up the ambush. Himmeth agreed with his suggestion and the unit began to deploy.

Till they were forced to vacate it due to Indian counter bombardment, Arhand had been a major Pakistani gun position. The shattered remains of several concrete bunkers, a gun pit, and the smouldering wreckage of three ammunition trucks bore mute testimony to the effectiveness of the Indian counter-bombardment fire.

Himmeth had ordered the company commanders to place physical barriers on the road. Not having anything else to do it with, the guardsmen piled up empty shell cases left behind by the Pakistani artillery battery on the road.

'We were tempted to put some live artillery shells also in the heaps,' Glucose gave a mischievous grin, 'but we were also worried about the damage they might cause to us, since our boys were deployed pretty close to the road block.'

By 0430 hours, the roadblock had been established and the companies deployed so that they were covering all approaches to and from Arhand. Between Alpha Company deployed to the south with the battalion HQ, and Charlie Company manning the road on the other side, the road had now become a death trap for any one coming down the road, from either side.

The *paltan* had barely finished deploying when a Pakistani one tonner came along. The driver speeded up when he saw the empty cases piled up on the road, and crashed through them easily. However, he was unable to escape the waiting guns of the guardsmen.

'I was amazed to see Himmeth take over one of my machine guns and start shooting at the Pakistani one-tonner,' said Paunchy, grinning at the memory. 'Himmeth was an excellent shot and had lightning reflexes. Did you know that he had failed the IMA entrance examination in 1947? However, he was so keen on joining the Army that he enrolled in the Jaipur State Forces. He did very well there. So much so that when he did finally join the IMA, in 1949, he was the only cadet who had already won a medal.'

Shortly thereafter, still unaware that the Indians had reached this far and were now in control of the road, another convoy of six vehicles came along. Within no time, the guardsmen had destroyed a jeep, one 1-tonner and five 3-tonners, as well as killed one Pakistani officer and thirty-one soldiers and captured another three. A little later, another small group came down the road and another six Pakistanis died in the ambush.

In addition to the actual physical damage that the Arhand roadblock inflicted on the Pakistanis, it also wreaked havoc on their morale, and must have also added to the confusion in the heads of their commanders. Unaware of the speed at which 4 Guards was moving forward, it must have seemed to the Pakistani higher command that the Indian Army was everywhere, and there were more of them than it had appeared initially.

With morning also came some Indian three tonners, as the rear echelons fetched up to the old Bravo Company location at Shyamnagar.

Loading up the dead and wounded, Midha started out for the ADS. For him, it was a poignant journey as they traversed the same ground on which the enemy had given them such a hard time. The debris of war was all around.

'We got held up at the bridge for a while. There were hundreds of our engineers clustered there. They were trying to see if the railway bridge could be re-configured to handle road traffic,' Midha added by way of explanation, 'because that would have allowed our vehicles to cut straight through and keep up with the advancing forces. The option was a hundred kilometre detour before the road swung back towards Ashuganj.'

Eventually, the injured guardsmen got through, taking their dead with them. A couple of hours later, they reached the ADS; the same journey that had taken them the whole night through slush and enemy fire.

'They were processing and cremating the dead bodies right then and there,' Midha sounded grim. Time had obviously not taken the sting out of the loss, as was evident. 'And those of us who were wounded ended up in the field hospital. I was attended to by Captain Vinay Kumar, who later joined our unit as the RMO.'

Delighted at the progress of operations, the Indian high command decided to seize the moment and exploit the gains made thus far. Sagat took the decision to maintain the speed of advance and the momentum of operations.

The Brahmanbaria-Comilla-Chittagong highway happened to be the main link between the two Pakistani divisions tasked for the defence of this area. With the guardsmen now in control of this highway, this vital artery had been snapped. Also, barring small pockets of resistance, a sixty-seventy mile wide corridor was now available for the Indian 4 Corps to advance on Meghna.

The original plan had been for 4 Corps to now turn and clear the area down towards Chittagong. This would give enough space for the interim Bangladeshi government to be established. Chittagong was also important since the American 7th Fleet was deployed off that coast and busy making threatening noises in support of its ally, Pakistan.

It is possibly now that Lieutenant General Sagat, seeing the opportunity open up for him, decided to launch a heliborne operation across the Meghna and head for Dacca, the bigger prize. And to do that, he needed to ensure that the isolated pockets of Pakistani troops in this corridor were cleared. This task fell to Bravo and Charlie companies of 4 Guards.

Consequently, 0900 hours of 6 December 1971 saw two platoons of Bravo Company under Major Kharbanda moving from Arhand to capture the Ujjainsar Bridge.

Held by a Pakistani section comprising mixed elements, the bridge was a vital link on the Comilla-Brahmanbaria road and its capture was critical to open the lines of communication to Agartala via Kasba.

The enemy offered only a token resistance and withdrew as soon as the preparatory artillery bombardment of their location began. They ran leaving behind large quantities of small arms and ammunition.

Simultaneously, Charlie Company under Tuffy Marwah moved to secure the concrete bridge at Sultanpur, three miles south of Brahmanbaria. This bridge was held by mixed elements of about company strength, but here also the enemy offered no resistance. They panicked and fled when Charlie Company was closing up to the bridge. Once again, they abandoned a large cache of arms and ammunition, including an RCL gun.

Charlie Company was still consolidating its position on the bridge when they were ordered to hand over the security of the bridge to the brigade following up behind them and fall back to Arhand.

But Charlie obviously had a lot of karma to resolve, because there was no respite for them. At 1600 hours, Charlie Company found itself heading for Saidabad, this time mounted on the nine tanks of 5 Independant Armoured Squadron that had reached Arhand around midday.

The only stop enroute was a brief skirmish at Tantar. Brief because the Pakistanis were in a hurry to cut and run.

In fact, by now, the Pakistanis were in serious disarray, spooked by the sight of Indian tanks or had simply decided to make a habit of it. Either way, they again abandoned Saidabad and ran without offering any resistance as Charlie Company closed in. Here also, they left behind a huge amount of arms and ammunition, including 105 mm artillery shells. However, they did manage to cause some damage to the Saidabad bridge before they vanished.

By 1800 hours, Saidabad had been invested and the remainder of the *paltan* closed in on it and finally, after six days of relentless engagement with the enemy, got a relatively peaceful night's rest.

DAY SEVEN

07 DECEMBER 1971

The seventh day passed spookily. Operations were flowing very rapidly since the situation was extremely fluid. Also, perhaps in the minds of the Indian brass, there was now some confusion as to how to exploit the gains made thus far.

By now it was clear that the Pakistanis were on the run and if the Indian forces seized the moment swiftly, there was a war to be won. However, no one had expected the Pakistanis to abandon their posts and make a run for it so easily. As their defences folded like a house of cards, the options that became available to the Indians increased geometrically. So did the confusion.

There was also the fact that by now, the attacking forces had moved so far and so fast that their administrative echelons were miles behind. It was merely a matter of time before ammunition and crucial warlike parts became critically low.

The attacking troops were so far out on a limb that one serious setback could well have brought the offensive to a permanent halt. All the Pakistanis had to do was to turn and fight. So fluid and delicately balanced was the situation that one serious dig-in and determined fight to the finish by the Pakistanis could easily have altered the course of the war.

However, Sagat was a man with an offensive bent of mind. As were Gonsalves, Mishra and the other commanders under him. They were willing to take the risk and pursue the retreating

Pakistanis, without giving them even a momentary respite, which could allow them to re-group.

It is doubtful that history would stop to take note of these confusion-ridden days, for both Indian and Pakistani commanders. But it was sometime during these fluid and fleeting hours that the fate of this war was decided.

Himmeth's band of guardsmen had cleared up most little pockets of Pakistani resistance in the corridor that the Indian Army had carved out for itself. Now it was as much a battle of the minds as it was on ground. The Pakistani will to fight was clearly wavering. It was at this delicate juncture that the Garud struck. Again.

'Early in the morning, we got orders to fall back to Akhaura, which we reached around noon,' Glucose said. 'But we had barely entered Akhaura when we were ordered to send one company back to Saidabad.'

Charlie Company again found itself being transported back to Saidabad and, on reaching there, was told to move on foot to Bidya-Kot, about forty kilometres away. They were tasked to find and secure a crossing for the rest of the unit across the Pagla river.

However, their plans were altered again, and Charlie Company, which was already across the Pagla river by now, was redirected to link up with the *paltan* at Rusulpur (near Brahmanbaria) on 08 December.

It was enroute to Rusulpur, when Tuffy Marwah was moving around with a party of six, trying to re-group his company, that the Pakistanis ambushed them.

Tuffy and his men reacted remarkably fast. He himself led the charge and killed three of the Pakistani soldiers, causing the rest of the ambush party to flee in panic. They even left behind five of their dead, and one MMG, one LMG and several rifles.

Orders changed yet again, and at 1600 hours, the unit was told to fall back to Arhand.

The first bit of news awaiting Himmeth when they reached Arhand was about Nahar Singh, his injured radio operator; despite prompt medical attention, he had lost seventy-five per cent of the action in the affected hand.

It was in a sombre mood that the colonel turned his mind to the war at hand.

'I remember Nahar often. Everytime I pick up a squash racquet, handle a golf club, or even pick up my spoon to eat... I remember that it is because of him that I am still able to do so...' his comment to Colonel Pyarelal left me feeling unaccountably sad.

DAY EIGHT

08 DECEMBER 1971

With the situation becoming increasingly fluid, Indian commanders at all levels were up and about, trying to get a grip on the real situation on ground. With the others, Mishra and Himmeth were also on the move.

'Perhaps that is why I got the call directly from the GOC (General Officer Commanding), General Gonsalves,' Paunchy explained. 'Himmeth must have been out of radio range. He certainly was for me when I tried to reach him to confirm the orders the GOC had given me.'

Aware that they would be facing highly fluid situations, the Indians had adopted an innovative method of communication.

'To speak to anyone from any unit, we simply had to first take the name of the officer commanding that unit and then the name of the person one wished to speak with,' Glucose explained. 'This made it possible for anyone from any unit to speak to anyone else, as long as they were in range.'

'This use of the name of the commander as the radio call sign of the unit led to considerable confusion in the Pakistani rank and file,' Naib Subedar Tirath Singh elaborated. 'Whilst I was being treated for my wounds at the ADS at Brahmanbaria, I found myself next to a Pakistani soldier who was also being treated by our doctors. For want of anything better to do, we got talking. I was thoroughly amused when he asked me what was this secret weapon called Himmeth, which he heard on the radio set just minutes before our attack on

Akhaura, and which continued to haunt them without respite for days after that.'

We all grinned with Tirath.

'That was really funny, and I would have loved to see his face when he actually found out what it meant, but I didn't want to let on how we were using radio communication,' Singh said.

Naib Subedar Tirath Singh

Also, to mask the meaning of their messages and their intent, the Indians had devised various code words for commonly used things and events.

'For example, *ghee* (hydrogenated oil) tins meant dead bodies and *atta ki bori* (sack of wheat flour) meant wounded,' said Paunchy as he went on to explain the logic also, since *ghee* was used for the cremation of bodies, which was why the code word was a logical choice. Also, like *atta ki bori*, carting back the wounded required a lot of manpower and effort.

'I was very surprised when I got the call from General Gonsalves,' Paunchy resumed. 'The GOC told me to rush to Brahmanbaria and meet him there. Firstly, I was surprised since the last I'd heard Brahmanbaria had yet to be cleared. Secondly, I had no idea what Himmeth would have to say to this order. '

An uncertain Paunchy first tried to reach Himmeth and when he failed to get through, called Brigadier Mishra and shared his concern. Mishra, who happened to be midway between Himmeth and Paunchy, passed their messages on to each other. Soon, Paunchy had the orders to go ahead to Brahmanbaria confirmed.

Within the hour, Alpha Company 4 Guards, with two troops of armour, was headed for Brahmanbaria. Lying between them was the Pagla river, swift flowing and deep.

Willy nilly, using country boats, they managed to get across. All but one of the five PT 76 tanks that they had captured from the Pakistanis at Akhaura sank almost as soon as they entered the river.

When Alpha Company finally entered Brahmanbaria, Paunchy found the GOC in the stadium. Parked right in the middle was his helicopter. Standing before him was Brigadier Tulli, the Commander of 73 Brigade.

Major General
B.F. Gonsalves PVSM

Major General Gonsalves looked very upset, and the brigadier very sheepish. While they finished their talk, I quickly caught up on events with the chopper pilots.

Like the Corps Commander, Lieutenant General Sagat, Gonsalves was also fond of aerial recons and was often found in the thick of battle with the leading elements of the Indian offensive.

That morning, he had been flying over Brahmanbari when he noticed there was no sign of any enemy activity. A second fly past reconfirmed this. Much to the horror of his pilots, Gonsalves ordered them to land.

They landed to find that the panicked Pakistanis had already abandoned Brahmanbaria on the night of 7th December and had fallen back to Ashuganj.

Whilst the rest of 4 Guards raced forward to link up, accompanied by the GOC, Alpha Company now began to scour and secure the town. One of their first stops was the HQ of Pakistani 14th Division. It was right beside the Pakistani HQ that they found sixty-nine bodies. They were in an embankment between the Divisional HQ and the stadium.

'There were sixty-three bodies of Bengalis, most probably Mukti Bahini chaps. And there were also six of our boys—men from 10 Bihar. Their hands had been tied behind their bodies and they had been shot in the head,' Paunchy's expression made it clear that the memory was still strong, and very disturbing. 'General Gonsalves was livid. I don't know what happened later, but I know he wanted to have General Abdul Majid, the Pakistani GOC 14 Division, tried for war crimes. After all, there is no way these executions could have taken place without his concurrence, or at least knowledge.'

It was also from the same HQ that Paunchy recovered what would prove to be a document of historic significance. This was a top secret (to be destroyed after reading) intelligence summary dated 12 March 1971, written by the GSO 1 of Pakistani Eastern Command. The Intelligence Summary made it abundantly clear that the show was over, and things in East Pakistan could now never go back to being what they had been earlier.

'It was obvious from this document that Pakistani high command were fully aware that East Pakistan had already spiralled out of control,' Paunchy looked incredibly saddened. 'This whole war … this huge waste of lives, on both sides, was so futile… Pakistan should have known better.'

But then history is replete with such examples. Rather than see the writing on the wall and accepting what the cards had dealt, the power-hungry Pakistani generals had chosen to wreak unspeakable atrocities on the hapless East Pakistanis, and had opted for a war with India. A war, that they would have known, they could never hope to win. They had tried it often enough.

Not too far away from Paunchy, my old friend Naik Jai Singh, who had carried his friend Subedar Rawat to safety, had made another find.

'One of my men came to me with a bag he had found in the Pakistani HQ. It was filled with Pakistani currency notes and silver ornaments,' Jai Singh explained. 'I think some Pakistani had probably been looting the local Bengalis. I felt very angry, and told him that soldiers don't do such things.'

On Jai Singh's orders, the guardsman threw the bag of loot into the pond they were standing beside. He had just done so when a Pakistani artillery shell landed into the pond.

'However, it did not explode,' Jai Singh said, as he shook his head in wonder. 'If it had exploded, both of us would have died that day. We took it as a sign from God that soldiers should never do such unspeakable things, like killing civilians in cold blood.'

Perhaps the Pakistanis should have paid heed to this. It may not have helped them win this war, but it would certainly have helped them lose it with more grace and dignity, as befits men of honour.

Soon the rest of the battalion began to build up on Brahmanbaria. The companies began to fan out and secure the town.

'It was pretty hilarious, the way the GOC had captured it single-handed,' Granthi's laugh was infectious. It came just in time and uplifted the solemn mood that had gripped the room.

Granthi's company began to secure the area allocated to them when they came across a wounded Pakistani soldier.

'He was rather badly wounded, and they had just abandoned him there, along with their dead,' Granthi told me. In a flicker, the mood turned grim again. 'He kept begging us not to leave him alone.'

The Delta Company medic gave the man first aid, whatever was available at his disposal at that time, but the Pakistani was too far gone. He died moments later.

'He was the enemy, but for some reason we felt some relief that he had not died alone,' Granthi said that simply, as nothing more than a statement of fact.

I sat back, dealing with the interplay of conflicting emotions that had been unleashed in me.

What is it about war? That it brings out the best in a man, just as easily as it unleashes the beast within. In one moment he is ready to kill and maim with bullet, bomb and bayonet… And then, in the very next, the same man has tears in his eyes as he remembers a fallen enemy. And he is relieved that he had at least not died alone, even though his own had abandoned him.

The Pakistanis had also left behind their dead.

'We were aware that the dead bodies would cause disease if left unattended,' Glucose stated. 'But the locals were absolutely petrified of the Pakistanis and not even ready to touch their bodies. We also knew that we could not cremate the bodies since Muslims do not burn their dead.'

It took considerable persuasion on the part of the Guards' officers before the locals finally dug a massive common grave and buried all the dead Pakistanis in it.

'As for our own bodies, we were moving so fast and had gone so far ahead of our admin echelons that we simply had to cremate them whenever there was a lull in the battle. We would then hand over the ashes and the man's identity tags to the Subedar Major, who was responsible to ensure they were sent back to the man's next of kin,' Glucose said this in a very matter of fact tone.

I empathized. It may sound callous, even cold-blooded, but that is the way of war. That, very often, is the way it ends for many soldiers: an unmarked grave, or an unceremonious cremation, in some alien land.

It was almost noon when Himmeth raced into Brahmanbaria town, at the helm of a captured Pakistani jeep.

By now Generals Sagat and Gonsalves had made up their minds to exploit the situation and pursue the Pakistanis relentlessly, without giving them any time or opportunity to settle down or regroup. They ordered Himmeth to resume advance on Ashuganj immediately.

It did not take long for Himmeth to gather his company commanders and give the orders for 4 Guards to begin its advance on Ashuganj.

The advance was to be carried out on two axes—Alpha Company moving on the right flank with squadron less two troops, and Bravo Company with the remaining two tank troops along the Brahmanbaria-Ashuganj road.

At approximately midday, Alpha Company and 5 Independent Armoured Squadron, alongwith the PT 76 tanks that had been captured from the Pakistanis, encountered the enemy at a railway junction five miles short of Ashuganj.

Paunchy, with a few other Alpha Company men, was riding atop the lead tank, which belonged to Major Shamsher Mehta, the Squadron Commander. They became aware of the Pakistani presence when the tank was fired upon. The anti-tank round luckily fell a few feet short, exploding harmlessly in the mud.

The infantrymen hurriedly dismounted, whilst Shamsher fired a couple of rounds into the grove from which they had been fired upon. Then, spraying the area with machine gun fire, he charged the grove, killing eleven Pakistanis and capturing the position.

Moving along the Brahmanbaria-Ashuganj road, Bravo Company, however, ran into heavy weather. They came under very effective fire and their advance stalled.

Himmeth coming up close behind with the rest of the battalion ordered Major Kharbanda, the Bravo Company Commander, to clear the opposition, secure the bridge, and resume advance.

Leading the assault through open paddy fields, Kharbanda was hit by an MMG burst at almost point blank range.

Guardsmen Ram Prasad and Ram Dayal Ram, both manning LMGs, saw their Company Commander fall. Kharbanda had fallen in the open and both realized that he would not survive for long. Moving forward immediately, they engaged and killed four Pakistanis, and silenced the bothersome MMG. That brought them momentary respite.

The respite would obviously be brief since the Pakistanis were showing signs of mustering for a counter-attack. Himmeth, who had also seen Kharbanda go down, alongwith several other men from Bravo Company, spotted the Pakistani movement and knew that an attack on Bravo Company was imminent.

This is what Himmeth said to Colonel Pyarelal about what happened next: 'I knew Kharbanda was gone if we did not do anything immediately. I requested the armour officer, Lieutenant Raj Mohan to attack. The youngster was audacious. He did not hesitate even for a second and lit into the enemy with his troop. Thank God for that, otherwise we would have had to write off Kharbanda for sure. Though Raj himself was also grievously wounded during the attack, but his action saved many lives that day.

Simultaneously, guided by Daljit the spunky FAC, the Indian Air Force carried out another very effective strike on the railway station, which literally broke the back of the Pakistani defenders. The three hundred odd Pakistanis holding the town fled without offering any serious resistance. They even left their wounded behind.

Amongst those captured by Bravo Company was a Pakistani officer of 12 Frontier Force.

'You are also from the Guards,' the Pakistani officer told Sahni. 'The guys who attacked us at Akhaura were also from the Brigade of Guards.'

'We are the same ones,' Sahni explained to him.

'Bloody hell! You guys move fast,' the Pakistani officer looked stunned. After a pause he added, 'Do you know, you guys were always so close behind us that everytime we stopped for a breather, your men would turn up.' He held up three fingers. 'Thrice!' Waving the fingers for emphasis, he said 'Thrice we had to leave our tea and run. How did you manage to move so fast?'

Even I wanted to know. I asked.

'I didn't say anything to him, but we were able to move fast because we improvised,' Granthi smiled. 'Now I don't even remember the kind of things we used to keep moving. Boats, canoes, makeshift rafts, bicycles, cycle rickshaws, horse carts, improvised sleds to pull stuff on… We used whatever we managed to commandeer.'

Just how effective they had been was clear from the fact that by now the psychological pressure on the Pakistanis was tremendous. And in the coming hours, it would continue to grow. Many more times would the Garud come knocking even before the tea finished brewing.

With that resistance cleared, 4 Guards now resumed advance on Ashuganj. However, it had caused Himmeth the loss of yet another of his company commanders. Rapidly running out of options, Himmeth now ordered Captain Sahni to take charge of Bravo Company.

The rest of the battalion was advancing behind Alpha and Bravo companies, but along the railway track.

'Every so often we would pass pockets of Pakistani stragglers,' Glucose commented. 'By now they had become thoroughly demoralized and were falling back helter-skelter.'

By 1500 hours, Dharamkot, situated on the railway line Brahmanbaria-Ashuganj, had also been taken. Here again, true to form, the Pakistanis withdrew without offering a fight, but they managed to demolish the bridge before the guardsmen could reach.

The blowing of this crucial bridge across the Meghna river was to have a major impact on the conduct of operations. This was one of the major reasons for General Sagat to launch a heliborne operation soon, a game-changing operation that would put a rapid end to the war.

Meanwhile, Midha had been sent back from the ADS in Agartala to the field hospital at Telliamora, about fifty kilometres back on the Dharmanagar-Agartala road. Eventually, he found himself on the operating table.

'They were taking care of the more serious casualties first, so that is why they took a while to get to me,' said Midha.

By now, two of his three major wounds had healed and only his hand was still giving some trouble. The X-rays showed that the splinters were still lodged inside.

'When the surgeon asked me if I wanted him to re-open the wounds and take out the splinters, I was not too keen to do that. The wounds seemed to be healing well, and even my hand was not really giving much trouble. Also, I did want to get back to my company. So I checked with the surgeon if the splinters would create any hassles for me later,' Midha elaborated.

'You can keep your war trophies if you want,' the surgeon had smiled and told him. 'They will eventually find their place in your body.'

'You still have them inside you? The splinters?' Honestly, I was surprised.

'Yes,' he held up the hand in a very matter of fact manner. 'And they don't really bother me. Only sometimes, when it is very cold and damp.'

Refusing to be sent back to the hospital at Guwahati, with the other more seriously wounded, Midha got himself discharged from the field hospital and on the morning of 8th December began to head back to his unit. The doctor didn't dissuade him either—everyone knows what a morale booster it is for any fighting unit to have its wounded re-join the battle.

But by now, the rest of the guardsmen had raced ahead. Though the aerial distance between Midha and the unit was barely twenty-five kilometres, there was no direct surface link. To get to them, Midha had to accompany a convoy, which would swing around some ninety kilometres via Comilla before it could get back towards Ashuganj.

'That's when I learnt that our engineers had been unable to improvise the railway bridge on the Akhaura-Ashuganj track,' Still sporting a bandage, Midha headed back to join his company. He was unaware that events were evolving very rapidly on the battlefield ahead. And caught firmly in the eye of the storm were the followers of the Garud—battered and bloody, but bashing on regardless.

Himmeth was setting out with his radio operators and escort party when one of the locals came running to warn him that the Pakistanis had been laying mines just before they had pulled out. Himmeth immediately told his security escort, Naik Panna Lal, to advance with caution and watch out for freshly dug mud, since the mines had apparently just been laid.

Naik Panna Lal had two sterling qualities. Firstly, he took his duty as the Commandant's protector seriously and literally, ensuring that no matter where they had to go, it was he who was walking directly in front of Himmeth.

Now this in itself was nothing anyone could find fault with if it had not been for his second sterling quality. Panna Lal had an exceedingly atrocious sense of direction. Often, Himmeth found him moving in directions that were totally at variance with where they were actually supposed to go.

'For a change, that day Panna Lal was headed in the right direction,' Himmeth had told Colonel Pyarelal. 'However, I am not sure he had heard a word of my warning about the land mines, because Panna Lal was moving as though he was on the parade ground; marching forward, steady and straight, without once looking down at the ground. However, God was watching over us that day; he saw us safely through the minefield.'

Reaching Ashuganj, Himmeth deployed his HQ in the mosque, a practice he had adopted in line with the logic that the Pakistanis would be unwilling to shell a place of worship. The logic had proved flawed since very soon the HQ was under very effective artillery fire.

Himmeth on radio at Ashhuganj

The Pakistani Artillery OP had taken up position on top of a grain silo and had a commanding view of the area around Ashuganj. He was able to bring down very effective fire, and Himmeth knew he would make life miserable for the guardsmen if left unattended. Once again he turned to Daljit and asked the FAC to call in an airstrike.

Unable to get a clear view of the target, Daljit decided to clamber on to an elevated position on top of the mosque. He had barely reached on top when the Pakistani gunners spotted him. Soon a blistering hail of fire began to rain down on him. Unmindful of it Daljit directed the strike.

'Daljit's airstrike was as effective as the previous one, if not as dramatic,' said Glucose with another quick grin. 'And despite the shelling he had been put through, two hours later, when Daljit finally dismounted from his precarious perch, he was as nonchalant and chirpy as ever.'

With the Pakistani Artillery OPs momentarily out of action, a lull set in and some kind of normalcy returned.

Also, by now, the Indian administrative vehicles had started to arrive. With the bridge across Lakhiya river (at Akhaura) now in Indian hands, essential supplies began to reach the unit. The engineers had also managed to float jeeps across. In addition, 4 Guards had commandeered a fire engine from the local fire brigade, so things had started looking up.

'In the supplies that reached us, thoughtfully packed by some kindly soul was a bottle of whiskey,' said Paunchy as he ran a hand over his namesake. 'That day, after a week of dirt and deprivation, we all managed to get a hot and reasonably pleasant dinner, and of course, a very welcome drink.'

Himmeth also took this opportunity to get his company commanders together for a briefing at the mosque.

However, the brief lull in the storm proved to be just that. The hot and reasonably pleasant meal had barely been swallowed when the Pakistani 105 mm artillery guns began yet again at around 2100 hours. Getting the range and location right was obviously not a challenge for them since they were playing in their own backyard.

'In all this mayhem, we were settling down for the night as best as we could when the call came from Brigade HQ,' Glucose explained. 'The Old Man was told to report to the commander at Brahmanbaria next morning and the unit was also told to be ready to move.'

Paunchy returned from the mosque to the location where his company was deployed to find his company senior JCO, Subedar Makhan, very agitated. Makhan complained that the engineer boys attached to Alpha Company were not listening to him and had now disappeared. Makhan assumed that they had lost their nerve due to the shelling and run away. It was only after some extensive hunting that they realized what had happened to the engineer men.

Alpha Company had suffered several direct hits. One of the enemy shells had landed right on top of the foxhole in which the engineers had taken shelter. So intense had been the blast that parts of their decimated bodies had been flung high up in the air, finally coming to rest in one of the trees overhead.

Pakistani artillery kept up the barrages through the night. Despite that, as ordered, 4 Guards geared up for the forthcoming move.

DAY NINE

09 DECEMBER 1971

About to depart for Brahmanbaria in his jeep, Himmeth called Paunchy, the senior-most company commander and officiating second-in-command, and told him to be ready to bring the battalion back to Brahmanbaria.

'Whom do I hand over charge to, sir?' Paunchy had queried, since they were now in contact with the enemy defences.

'You don't worry about that. 18 Rajput and 10 Bihar are coming up now, and 73 Brigade is moving in from the flank,' was the reply he received.

A few hours later, at about 1000 hours, Paunchy received orders from Himmeth to get the battalion back to Brahmanbaria as fast as possible.

'That's why we just got up and moved out. But it was not a very good decision by the brass,' Paunchy said, while shaking his head mournfully. 'Later, when 18 Rajput and 10 Bihar reached Ashuganj, they literally walked into hell. The Pakistanis blasted them with pretty much everything they had, and both units suffered very heavy casualties.'

I was watching him closely; looking for any signs of thank-God-it-was-not-us. There were none. I realized he was merely telling the story, as objectively as he could.

It was only when the battalion had gone a few miles from Ashuganj that Subedar Makhan realized that in all the confusion, they had forgotten to retrieve the bodies of the engineer men from the trees.

Meanwhile, Himmeth had reached the Brigade Commander at about 0600 hours on 09th December 1971, and was told that he had to accompany General Sagat Singh and the Brigadier for an aerial recon. The trio took off at 0800 hours in an Alliot, with Sagat sitting in front with the pilot and Mishra and Himmeth in the rear seat.

Aerial recon with Lieutenant General Sagat Singh GOC 4 Corps

'Never having viewed land from the air before, I was quite lost, but Sagat had a very clear idea of what he was looking for. It is now that Sagat revealed his intention to clear the Meghna river with a heliborne operation and push ahead to Dacca. I was thrilled, since my presence here obviously implied that my unit would be involved in this historical operation,' Himmeth's recollections to Colonel Pyarelal said it as eloquently as anyone could.

'We finally found what we thought was the ideal location for such an operation—at Raipura, west of the Meghna. The joyride was a novel experience for me, but turned out to be more than what I'd bargained for. Especially when, on the way back, Sagat decided to take a closer look at certain enemy positions. Much to my horror, he decided to go down as low as a hundred feet. I don't know what it is with senior officers... Did they all believe that the bullet meant for them had not yet been made by the enemy? It did not seem to perturb the General much, not even when we were fired upon and Brigadier Mishra missed losing his head by a mere three inches. I'd heard stories about Sagat and his air escapades. The number of times he was shot at had become a standing joke. So often had it happened that the joke was that he had changed wounded pilots more frequently than he had changed his shoes,' Himmeth had continued to recall.

'On the flip side was Sagat's undeniable (and positively endearing) quality of always being upfront at the point of a decision. Of being able to see, judge and decide rapidly what we needed to do next. I personally believe that this trait of his had a major role to play in our winning this war so swiftly. And this was not the first time he was pulling off such a caper; Sagat had a penchant for rapid manoeuvres. Commissioned in the 3rd Gorkha Rifles, of which he commanded two battalions, Sagat Singh had also commanded India's first and only Parachute Brigade, the 50th. It was men from this brigade that, led by him, had not only played a pivotal role in the liberation of Goa, but also been the first to enter Panjim on 19 December 1961,' Himmeth had said.

I pondered over all this for a moment. How much of Himmeth's sentiment was personal, and how much professional? Did it matter? After all, perception is reality? So, what is reality?

Shrugging, I returned to Colonel Pyarelal's notes of Himmeth's reminiscences of that aerial recon.

Luckily, we all managed to return to Brahmanbaria intact. After some deliberations, General Sagat decided to go firm on Raipur as the landing place.

General Sagat Singh – Visiting the troops at the front line

A little later, Brigadier Mishra gave me the orders; 4 Guards would again be leading the charge. I was thrilled at the confidence shown in us by the top brass. However, I must confess, having seen the mighty Meghna, I was happy that Sagat had given us choppers and not expected us to swim across it. He could easily have done so. I don't think the General knew the word 'impossible'!

I hastened to reach my HQ. Still not fully sure why, but I knew that something momentous was going down. Perhaps I did not fully realize the impact our heliborne operation was going to have on the outcome of the war. Neither I am sure, did the Pakistanis, else they would have fought us tooth and nail when we landed.

'The Old Man was with the Brigade Commander in the stadium when the battalion reached Brahmanbaria at about 1300 hours. Himmeth was all charged up and beaming when he told us that the unit would be heli-landed across the Meghna in a few hours,' Glucose gave a boyish grin when he said that. 'I don't think he realized that none of us had had even a few hours of sleep ever since we had crossed the border eight days ago. Or that our ranks had been sorely depleted due to casualties. However, strangely enough, none of us objected to that either. Primarily because we had seen Himmeth slog through everything shoulder to shoulder with us, and we were all aware that the Old Man never asked us to do anything he himself was not ready for,' He continued.

4 Guards getting ready to breach the Meghna river

Hearing that, also the manner in which it was delivered, gave me a better sense of what Granthi had said earlier, that if he ever had to go to battle again, he would want to do so under Himmeth's leadership. It also gave me a more precise sense of how wide a shadow this aptly named man had cast over the battalion he had led.

'That's true,' Glucose interrupted my thoughts. 'I hadn't seen Himmeth so excited in a long time. No one got a minute to rest. Orders were issued and as usual there was so much to be done …

ammunition, food, weapons, casualties, re-distribution of men and equipment… We had no idea where the day went.'

'It's all on record,' Paunchy was beaming with pride. 'The entire battalion was launched into a heliborne operation with only four hours notice.' He handed me a sheaf of letters that had been written by several commanders, to Himmeth. I glanced through them; each had a story to tell. So much so that I immediately decided they needed to be a part of this book. That is why you will find them at the end of the book.

'And mind you,' Paunchy wagged an impatient, important finger when I looked up from the letters, 'we had been in constant contact with the enemy for eight solid days by now. We had taken many casualties including several key officers, and the boys were tired as hell. But inspite of all that, we were ready to go, at the impossibly short notice of four hours.'

The first sortie of ten MI4 choppers landed in Brahmanbaria stadium by 1500 hours.

'We gathered the men and quickly explained the basics of heliborne operations to them,' Granthi explained. 'Those who wanted to, were given the opportunity to try out the mounting and dismounting drill. Especially the dismounting drill, since we knew that we would most probably be dismounting from the choppers in the face of the enemy.'

'To be fair, in the year gone by, whilst the unit had been operating in the Mizo hills, we had carried out a number of heliborne operations against the Mizo hostiles,' Glucose pointed. 'Though none of these operations had been on as large a scale as the one we were embarking on right now, but they had given the boys a basic idea of how to operate in such conditions.'

The drills were being explained to the men when the first hiccup happened. Squadron Commander Sandhu, who was in charge of the sortie, learnt that they would be landing at an unsecured landing ground across the Meghna. Immediately, there was some hesitation on his part. Perhaps he had been affected by some bad experience during the earlier Silhit operations.

Luckily, before matters could escalate, Group Captain

Chandan landed and took charge. At 1600 hours, the first assault wave was ready to go.

'It had been decided that my Company would be leading the charge across the Meghna,' Paunchy was still beaming with pride, as though it was happening all over again. 'The Old Man decided to accompany us in the first sortie. When we were getting into the chopper, we saw Group Captain Chandan already ensconced inside. Colonel Himmeth was surprised and asked him what he was doing there. I can never forget Chandan's cheeky grin as he replied that he was coming along to ensure we Army footsloggers got out of the choppers fast enough. None of us said anything. There was no need to. It was courage such as this that had kept us going all these days. It was this attitude, displayed by commanders at all levels that would win the war for us.'

Air Vice Marshal Chandan Singh, MVC, VrC, AVSM, (Retd.) M.B.I.M (London)

Though the MI4 chopper usually carries between eight to twelve men with their full battleload, that day the guardsmen had crammed in fourteen to sixteen men in each. In addition, there were also two or three Mukti Bahini guides-cum-porters. Luckily, the choppers were flying out from the stadium so they had enough space to take off. Had they been forced to take off vertically, it is doubtful they could have lifted so many men.

The thirty minute long flight across the Meghna seemed to take forever.

The rear boom doors were open during the flight so the guardsmen could see the river down below.

'In full spate, the Meghna looks more like a sea than a river,' Puanchy remarked. 'It was an endless expanse of water and no matter where one looked, one could not see the other bank of the river. No unit could have hoped to get across it in any other way and reach the other end as a cohesive, tactically viable, fighting force.'

This was especially true considering the time frame; the Indians did want to keep the Pakistanis on the run and ensure they were not able to fall back in an orderly fashion and defend Dacca.

Despite the two Gnat fighters flying a Combat Air Patrol (CAP), to provide the required protection from enemy air, tension was high, and it was visible in the way men gripped their weapons. The roar of the rotors was an absolute conversation killer. At yet another level, time seemed to move incredibly fast. Soon, Raipura was in sight. Stress was building up as they swept in to land. Every man on board knew this was the most vulnerable moment. Even a couple of Pakistanis with rifles could have inflicted a terrible toll. Until such time the guardsmen managed to get their boots on the ground and secure it.

Group Captain C.S. Sandhu, VrC, VM

That is what (then) Squadron Leader Sandhu had been apprehensive about earlier.

'It is so easy for you Army guys to say: "Get me across the river and land me there at night." But let me give you an idea of the complexities involved,' Sandhu, now retired, but still standing tall and upright, every bit the officer even today, elaborated. 'Please remember, that most of my pilots had not been trained for night flying, and in those days, choppers had no fancy night flying equipment. Moonlit nights were one thing, but dark nights were totally out of the question. Navigation lights on choppers were out of the question if secrecy had to be maintained, and there used to be no landing lights waiting for us at the other end since we would be going into enemy territory. To add to it, in such operations, generally, strict radio silence is enforced.

So everything had to be done by the pilots relying only on their senses, and coordination with each other.'

I tried to visualize the picture he was painting. To be fair, it did sound dark and gloomy.

On that fateful evening, when 4 Guards took off, the chopper pilots had trained to the extent that each one of them was able to reach the exact same spot at distances of sixty kilometres, at precise intervals of sixty seconds. This would deliver rich dividends today.

Heli-landing across the Meghna river – the decisive blow that broke the back of the Pakistani Army

'Remember that each chopper was carrying far more than the permissible load, because we did want to ensure you guys would reach with your heavy weapons and ammunition,' Sandhu resumed talking when he saw me nod. 'We had to cover dozens of kilometres and find the exact spot in darkness so the navigation and plotting had to be spot on,' he leaned forward to emphasize. '180 kmph meant a hundred and eighty kmph. Not hundred seventy-nine; and not hundred eighty-one. Because with every passing mile, the effect of the smallest error would get magnified. Now, once we did manage this near impossible task of reaching the right place, each chopper had between fifteen to twenty seconds to hover, off-load and be away, otherwise the next one would smash into it. Do also remember, with visibility almost nil and the bird in front not showing any lights,' another emphatic finger jab, 'no one could see the guy in front.'

Since the landing ground had not been prepared or secured, the first flight of choppers did not land; they hovered about a foot above the ground, and the guardsmen jumped out. Despite not having much experience of such operations, the men were out of the birds in fifteen to thirty seconds, while the choppers headed back to get the next lot.

'Luckily, our boys had some prior experience of flying with the MI4,' Paunchy explained. 'The MI4 door has a very tricky catch and there is a particular trick to opening and closing it. To make matters worse, the tail rotor is very low, so one has to be careful when de-planing. You have to move left or right as soon as you get off, else it can chop you up. In fact, that is what happened to one of the 10 Bihar boys.'

Now, even with men on ground to light up the way for the next set of choppers, the situation got only marginally easier.

'We had experimented with all kinds of lights for such operations. But in the end, what worked best were empty food tins filled with sand soaked in kerosene,' Sandhu smiled at the incredulous expressions all around. 'Yes, they would keep burning even with the downdraft from the chopper blades hammering at them.'

Pilot Officer Daljit Singh was one of the first men out of the choppers. He, as was his habit, rapidly took in the lay of the land, identified the best position for himself in case he had to direct an airstrike. In the event that the enemy tried to interfere with the landing ground. It was also his job to ensure he lit up the way for the next in-bound sortie of choppers.

However, the Gods of War were kind, and the guardsmen encountered no enemy at Raipura. What they did meet was a throng of ecstatic locals who proved invaluable in helping to unload the choppers and also helped to carry their stores and ammunitions.

Within minutes of landing, Alpha Company had fanned out and secured the landing ground. With this major worry resolved, as ordered by Himmeth, Paunchy now headed towards Methikanda with a radio operator and a couple of men, to check out what lay ahead.

Paunchy had been specifically tasked to carry out a quiet patrol. However, the Indian military planners had forgotten to plan for a critical and unexpected factor—the exuberant and vociferous Bengali locals.

It scarcely took any time before Paunchy's men had been surrounded by a mob of ecstasic locals. Joyous shouts of *Joy Bangla, Joy Hindustan* and *Joy Indira Gandhi* shook the area around.

This throng burgeoned and grew louder with every passing moment. The atmosphere prevalent was more like a country fete than a deadly military operation deep behind enemy lines.

The Pakistanis, about a company worth of irregulars, the East Pakistan Civil Affairs Force (EPCAF) and Razakars, dug in at Methikanda about two kilometres away would have heard it. They did not respond, but their counterparts located at their main defensive position in Ashuganj did attempt to disrupt the landing with artillery fire for a good five to ten minutes. However, the landing ground had been chosen with due consideration for this threat and their shells landed almost a kilometre short.

While choosing the landing ground, General Sagat had also borne in mind the fact that the Pakistani GOC 14 Infantry Division, who was directing most of the Pakistani war effort in this area, was located at Bhairab Bazar, not too far away. Co-located with him was a troop of the light Pakistani Chaffe tanks. It was imperative to ensure that neither of them could interfere with an unsecured landing by the guards.

The risk was high since even a few lightly armed men could have dealt havoc on the inbound choppers.

Dusk was falling when Paunchy, accompanied by a radio operator and a couple of men, reached the outskirts of Methikanda, surrounded of course by a raucous mob of Bengalis. A company of Pakistanis held Methikanda, about two or two-and-a-half kilometres away from the landing ground.

By now, the Pakistanis deployed at Methikanda were so badly spooked that they had loaded up all their stuff in a railway wagon and were using locals to push it along the track, rapidly making their way towards Narsinghdi.

'Though they were really far away, we fired a couple of rounds in their direction to encourage them to keep moving,' Paunchy laughed. 'Of course we were mindful of the locals pushing the wagon, and therefore aimed high.'

In any case, the Pakistanis had had enough. They withdrew towards Narsinghdi, leaving Methikanda to the guardsmen.

At the landing ground, Colonel Himmeth settled down to wait for the rest of the *paltan* to fly in. The plan had been to complete the build-up as soon as possible, and then resume the advance. However, shortly thereafter, a message was received that there would be a delay before the next sortie landed due to some problems at the other end.

It was around 2300 hours that the sorties resumed.

It is hard to forget Daljit running around organizing the makeshift landing lights. Of the thunderous roar of ten choppers coming in out of the darkness, only switching on the lights when they were barely hundred feet off the ground. Of Daljit standing there like Misa, billowed and buffeted by the downdraft, and illuminated eerily by the flashing strobe-like landing lights, as he cajoled the choppers in.

Going over Colonel Pyarelal's notes, I could imagine the sight Himmeth had painted. I could almost hear the volley of shouted orders and see the heart-warming sight of guardsmen racing out of the choppers, guns at the ready.

Five times, the choppers returned that night and by 0300 hours on 10 December 1971, the last guardsman had crossed the Meghna.

Just to give you an idea of the intricacies of a heliborne operation: a MI4 carries between eight to twelve men, depending on the combat load being carried. In the six sorties (of ten choppers per sortie), 4 Guards managed to get about six hundred men across. They also ferried across four MMGs, four of their 81 mm mortars, two 106 mm RCL guns, their entire complement of 1st and 2nd line ammunition, and a troop of 120 mm heavy mortars.

Meanwhile, a few kilometres away, at Methikhanda, Paunchy went to ground and settled down to wait for Granthi to link up with him.

Methikanda was a critical link (more of a railway yard, actually) on the Ashuganj-Dacca railway line. Its importance lay in the fact that it lay west of the Meghna, and hence could be used to move cargo by road via Ashuganj, as well as via rail. Mehtikanda could also be used for cargo that was carried along the Meghna and could be off-loaded in the vicinity.

Strict radio silence was in place, so Paunchy had no way of knowing what was happening back at the landing ground. However, he was within earshot and his worry began to mount when no choppers could be heard coming in for a while. Eventually, he could hear the choppers again, but there was still no sign of Granthi, who was supposed to link up with him.

As the hours ticked away, and the dawn of 10th December inched closer, Paunchy was concerned about Granthi's absence.

DAY TEN

10 DECEMBER 1971

Unknown to Paunchy, things were not going very well for Delta Company. They had landed safely alongwith the rest of the battalion, and immediately on landing, as per Himmeth's plan, had set out to link up with Paunchy at Methikhanda.

Delta Company was barely a mile away from the landing ground when, silently, without any warning whatsoever, the deadliest enemy known to any Army anywhere in the world struck—a young officer trying to make sense of a map.

'Look,' Paunchy explained, 'I don't blame the poor guy. It can happen to anyone. I mean, even I have gotten lost. But that night, it was the limit. I was sitting there, almost alone. There were just a handful of us, deep inside enemy territory, and Granthi didn't show up and I was sitting there cursing him.'

Unfortunately for Granthi, Paunchy's curses were the least of his worries when he misread the map and took a wrong turn. Unknown to him, Granthi was now headed straight into the lion's den—the main Pakistani 14 Division defences at Bhairab Bazar.

As soon as 4 Guards landed across the Meghna, the final major hurdle to Dacca had been crossed. The Indians knew that the bulk of the Pakistani Eastern Army stood between them, un-blooded and well equipped. But they also knew they had the Pakistanis on the run. The psychological war had already been won: the Pakistani brass had been tested and found wanting.

Perhaps the Pakistanis had been misled by the experiences of the 1965 Indo-Pak conflict, where the Indian Army had conceptually fought many battles with limited aims and small manouevres. They may have expected this conflict to be a replay of the previous one. It is certain that they had not expected the Indians to have Dacca as the final objective.

'And certainly, they had not expected us to maintain the kind of speed that we did, considering the arduous and treacherous terrain we had to navigate. In either case, we had them on the run,' said Glucose. Having been the adjutant during the operations, he had obviously been most exposed to the thinking of the Indian high command. 'Once we had broken past the outer crust, the Pakistanis had little in depth to contain us.'

Sagat's decision, once he decided to use heliborne forces to cross the Meghna, was the final nail in the Pakistani coffin; it sealed the deal for them. They lost all hope of winning the war, and withdrew rapidly. They were now as shaky in the mind as on the ground. The only thing left to be delivered now was the coup de grace.

The panic in the minds of the Pakistani leadership was evident from the message sent by General Niazi to the Pakistani Army HQ: Enemy heli-dropped one brigade at Narsinghdi. Keeping this in view, it was hardly surprising that on 9th Decemeber 1971, General Yayha Khan approached the United Nations pleading for a ceasefire.

The first nail in this coffin was driven in completely inadvertently. And that was by the misguided Captain Surinder Singh and his mistake with the map.

Granthi only realized the gravity of his situation when he blundered into the main Pakistani defences and all hell broke loose.

'My detachment was now with Delta Company,' Mukund came to life suddenly. 'We were moving from Raipura to Methikanda to link up with Major Chandrakant when we got lost. We only realized something had gone wrong when enemy artillery began to rain down on us. They had told us back at Raipura that the enemy had already withdrawn from Mehtikhanda to Narsinghdi, so we knew something had gone seriously wrong. The firing was very intense, and to make it worse, the Pakistani Artillery OP directing the fire was really good and the shells landed spot on. With no time to dig in, we scattered and took cover as best we could.'

Gurdev and Mukund, both mortar platoon men, hunkered down in a fold of land, trying to take cover as best possible.

'When the firing finally eased off, we started moving again,' Mukund's voice had gone soft. 'But Gurdev did not get up. I nudged him, but he did not move. That is when I realized he had been hit.'

'Did you know him well?' I asked, when it became obvious that he was not going to say any more.

'Of course, I did. We were from the same village,' Mukund nodded, still pensive. 'I even met his family later, after the war. He didn't have any children, which is good, but his wife went through a very bad time afterwards. She, too, died a little later. I am not sure exactly when, but I remember it was not too long after the war.'

This time it was I who felt the compelling need for silence. Excusing myself, I walked out for a breath of fresh air. I was contemplating the Army widow's legacy. Finally I knew I had to get back. To the war that was still alive in the handful of men waiting for me in that room.

Granthi eventually managed to extricate his men and get back on track. He eventually found his way back to Methikhanda and linked up with Paunchy in the early morning. By now Paunchy was fuming.

'Although, as it turned out, in a way, Delta Company getting lost and blundering into the Pakistani defences turned out to be a real boon,' Glucose's smile was a strange blend of pleasure and pain. 'The Pakistanis had been hearing our choppers coming back again and again. They couldn't have really known how many choppers there were or how many sorties we eventually carried out. That's why when Granthi blundered into their defences, they simply assumed that we had gotten a brigade across the Meghna and this was a deliberate attempt by us to probe their defences.'

'Precisely!' expressed Paunchy as he thumped the arm of his chair firmly. 'It didn't help that they were already pretty spooked by now. So deep had the siege mentality set in, and so used to had they become to finding our troops suddenly emerge in their rear, that Granthi's walking into their defences seriously sent the wind up their sails.'

The dawn of 10th December 1971 saw 4 Guards firming up at Methikanda. They were still doing so, when, at about 1000 hours, a chopper landed on the roof of a school building in Methikhanda and out came the Corps Commander Lieutenant General Sagat, 57 Mountain Division Commander Major General Gonsalves and Brigadier Mishra, the 311 Mountain Brigade Commander.

They arrived like the proverbial three kings from the Orient. However, instead of gold, frankincense and myrrh, they had brought along a big pile of oranges.

'Usually, the arrival of so much brass cannot be anything other than a pain, but not when one is in the field, in the thick of a war,' Naik Hoshiar Singh, who had been Himmeth's radio operator throughout the sixteen days, spoke up all of a sudden, taking me by surprise. A rather taciturn man, he had been silent all this while. 'We were quite thrilled to see our senior commanders out there in the front lines with us. It made us realize that they cared for us,' he said further.

Glucose gave a big nod, and said, 'The first thing they asked us was if we needed any help.'

Fortunately, the Pakistanis had failed to contest the fly-in across the Meghna or the landing at Raipura. In fact, during the entire operation, 4 Guards encountered no opposition from the enemy barring Delta Company, and its unfortunate encounter when it blundered into the main Pakistani defences at Bhairab Bazar. Other than this and some aching hands caused by some seriously enthusiastic locals, it had been smooth sailing till then.

Perhaps the Pakistanis had been deluded about the importance of the heliborne operation. Or perhaps they had been too caught up in dealing with the holding attack that was launched by the balance of 311 Mountain Brigade on Ashuganj and Bhairab Bazar which lies contiguous to Ashuganj, but on the western banks of the Meghna.

This holding attack launched in conjunction with the heliborne operation may have led Pakistani GOC 14 Infantry Division to believe that Sagat would continue to try and attempt a surface crossing of the Meghna, somewhere in the vicinity of Ashuganj. This in turn would have made it imperative for the Pakistanis to try and deny the Indian forces the general area of Bhairab Bazar. So that is where the Pakistanis concentrated their forces.

'Consequently, we were in pretty good shape. Well, as good as could be expected, considering we had been in non-stop contact with the enemy for nine continuous days now,' said Glucose. 'Nonetheless, like he mentioned,' he nodded towards Hoshiar Singh, 'seeing our top brass with us at the front line, and this gesture on their part, went down very well with the men. Not everyone may have gotten an orange, but everyone certainly felt great.'

The guardsmen's morale, which was already high, soared. They showed their appreciation by giving a return gift of a handful of bananas to the brass. Bangladeshi bananas are quite delicious, and bearing this priceless gift, the generals departed after giving 4 Guards their latest orders—to advance and secure Narsinghdi. And hold it open for the balance of the brigade and an artillery battery to be heli-landed.

'Along with the oranges, Sagat had also gotten maps of the Dacca area,' Paunchy said with a wry smile. 'On these maps, the routes to Dacca had been clearly marked. This was the first indicator we got that Dacca would most likely be our next objective.'

Himmeth had gone to see the generals off to their chopper when he remembered something critical and told the corps commander: 'And since you did ask, sir, we could do with some wireless batteries. We've just run out of the last set.'

An hour after Sagat left, the required wireless batteries were air delivered to the guards.

'It was these little things that made so much of a difference,' Glucose remarked. 'That let us know the brass genuinely cared for us and worried about our needs.'

It was Sagat's free roaming over the complete theatre of operations, I read Colonel Pyarelal's notes later than night, and his uncanny ability to be there, at the point of decision, that not only made him endearing, but also helped make him the right one to guide us to victory.

Himmeth was aware of the value of keeping the enemy under pressure. That was also possibly the best way to keep Indian casualties down. Thus, it was imperative that the momentum of operations be maintained at all costs.

Eager to hit Narsinghdi at the earliest, the guards kicked off.

The move was a sight to behold. Every possible type of vehicle (manual and powered) that the guardsmen could lay their hands on had been put to use. However, of these there were not too many and the bulk of the battleload fell on a willing stream of Mukti Bahini porters. The porters took the guardsmen forward in relays, leap-frogging from one village to the other. They were a merry bunch, chanting and singing songs as they moved. Since the porters changed with every village, so did the song. What did remain constant were the cries of *Joy Bangla, Joy Hindustan, Joy Mujib-ur-Rehman* or *Joy Indira Gandhi*. The cries came at regular intervals. The atmosphere was more like a wedding procession than an Army advancing to wage war on the enemy.

The wedding procession came to an abrupt halt when the leading platoon of Bravo Company encountered the enemy at the rail bridge, which spanned one of the many minor rivers. Once again, the thunder of guns shattered the countryside.

The platoon firmed in and maintained contact with the Pakistanis, who made several attempts to dislodge the platoon, but failed.

By evening, the remainder of Bravo Company had built up on this platoon and they kept the enemy under constant pressure. This prevented the Pakistanis from destroying the bridge, which was a vital objective since it would make life easier for the administrative echelons to keep up with the striking forces.

Meanwhile, Charlie Company had moved north towards Bhairab Bazar. They deployed along the Meghna south of Bhairab Bazar and covered 19 Punjab, as it crossed the river in a bewildering variety of country boats and ferries.

DAY ELEVEN

11 DECEMBER 1971

After successfully helping 19 Punjab cross the Meghna, Charlie Company again returned to Methikanda, and on 11 December 1971, along with the rest of the battalion, advanced on Narsingdi. Barring minor skirmishes, 4 Guards advanced unchecked.

'By now we were accompanied by several hundred locals, who helped carry the ammunition of the heavy mortar troop accompanying us, as well as the 81 mm mortar ammunition,' Maneck added.

By now the Pakistanis were playing to form, and most of them had already fled Narsinghdi.

'At Narsingdi, a fairly large industrial town, we received a heroes' welcome, and were served with sweets and fruit,' Granthi paused, then grimaced. 'However, things turned ugly when some irate citizens captured a handful of Razakars and executed them. By the time we came to know, it was too late to stop them.'

'And have no doubts about it, the people were very miffed with the Pakistani Army. They had been badly brutalized all these years, and were aching to take revenge,' Tuffy elaborated.

With the railway bridge now in the hands of Bravo Company, and with Charlie Company securing the East Pakistan Roadways bus stand and the fire station next to it, the battalion's transport problems were now largely resolved.

The other companies, meanwhile, had moved to secure the landing ground for the rest of the brigade to fetch up.

Paunchy had just driven up to the landing ground, where 10 Bihar and the Brigade HQ was landing, in a commandeered tuk-tuk (auto rickshaw), when a small aircraft swept in and landed in the field close by. Paunchy was delighted to see Major Bhargava jump out. The duo had not met since the days of the aerial recon over Akhaura that Bhargava had so merrily taken the Guards officers on.

'Boss, I need some petrol,' was Bhargava's demand.

Paunchy should have, by now, gotten used to Bhargava's eccentric requests, but he couldn't help laughing. 'You've run out?' Bhargava replied with a sheepish nod. 'That thing runs on petrol?' Paunchy indicated towards the aircraft. A Bhargava-special grin this time. 'Well, I don't have any, but you take this tuk-tuk and go with my man to town. Tuffy is there. He will give you all the petrol you need,' was Paunchy's offer.

Sure enough, twenty minutes later, Bhargava returned laden with some jerrycans and topped up his aircraft. A merry wave later, he was off.

He had barely cleared off when Group Captain Chandan landed in the next chopper, saw Paunchy, and waved him over. 'I need some transport. I need to do some recon. I have to find a landing ground for our Caribou.'

'The tuk-tuk was becoming very popular,' Paunchy grinned. 'In fact, the very next day, our GOC, General Gonsalves, used it as his flag car.'

Minutes later, Chandan had headed off in the tuk-tuk, with a couple of Alpha Company men as escorts.

'The area was far from clear,' Paunchy explained. 'There were pockets of Pakistanis holding out here and there. Not to mention the stragglers and runaways who were trying to fall back to their rear positions. But things were very fluid and crazy by now. Everyone was improvising on a minute-to-minute basis, even though it was quite risky.'

Paunchy had no idea how prophectic these words would soon prove to be. Done with the landing ground, he returned to his company, which was scouring Narsinghdi town.

Most of the Pakistani defenders had managed to extricate themselves and had fled Narsinghdi. However, a handful of them had taken shelter in a powerhouse located to the west of the town.

'It was an electricity sub-station and about sixteen or seventeen of them had gone to ground in it,' said Paunchy, the Alpha Company Commander. The powerhouse fell in his beat, and thus also the task of clearing it.

Protected by a triple layer of barbed wire, the powerhouse was an easily defensible position. The bunkers in it were solid concrete; possibly fortified to ensure it could be held against the Mukti Bahini for extended durations.

An intial probe to jitter the enemy out met with no success. Then Paunchy's men tried to lob grenades and scare the Pakistanis into coming out. That was going on when a Pakistani grenade landed about ten feet away from Paunchy.

'It should have taken care of a few of us, but fortunately the damn thing didn't explode,' Paunchy said. Realizing these half-measures were not working, Paunchy decided to organize a proper attack on the sub-station.

The first attack by a platoon was beaten back with heavy casualties before they could get past the barbed wire fence.

Alpha Company re-grouped. By now, someone had managed to locate a wire cutter and though under fire, the guardsmen were able to cut a hole in the fence.

'The bunker in front was giving us hell,' Paunchy explained. 'So I asked Guardsman Imam Singh to neutralize it.'

Imam Singh was a simple soul from Bihar.

'What do I do with it?' he asked, holding up the grenade handed to him.

'You throw it in that bunker,' Paunchy pointed out. 'After pulling out the pin,' he added by way of explanation. Then, just to ensure he had covered the final relevant detail, Paunchy added, 'Pull the pin out just before you throw it into that bunker.'

Without hesitation, Imam Singh marched across to the bunker and tossed the grenade inside. And he pulled out the pin just before doing so.

That sorted out the first problem for Alpha Company.

'Such men are remarkable. We may jest about them, but it is men like Imam Singh on whose shoulders victories are won,' Paunchy's tone was filled with pride. Then came sorrow. 'I can never forget how he died.'

Paunchy was holding open the gap in the barbed wire fence and helping his men through it one by one. Imam was halfway through the fence when Paunchy felt his body shudder.

'There was a gurgle and I felt my hand on his shoulder go wet. That is when I realized he had been hit. I pulled him back, but by then he was already gone.'

Removing his body from the gap, Paunchy helped the next man through and then followed him into the breech. The Pakistanis greeted them with a steady stream of fire. One of the bullets hit the ground next to Paunchy, and ricocheted up, striking him in the leg.

'Luckily it was not a direct hit, or else it would definitely have shattered the bone. As a matter of fact, all I felt initially was a pinch and some discomfort. I only realized I had been shot when I touched my leg and my hand came away all bloody,' he said.

By now, light was fading and visibility had dropped. So Himmeth ordered Alpha Company to stand down for the time being. Paunchy pulled back.

The RMO, Captain Sutradhar, aware that Paunchy was not likely to be the most patient of patients, gave him a morphine shot as soon as he reached the medical aid post.

Immediately, on receipt of confirmation that 4 Guards had secured Narsinghdi, HQ 311 Mountain Brigade and 10 Bihar commenced their fly-in across the Meghna. This time, the landing ground was just south of Narsinghdi.

One of the first to land was the Commander Brigadier Mishra. Within minutes of his arrival, Mishra began to assess the situation with Himmeth.

DAY TWELVE

12 DECEMBER 1971

Tuffy and Charlie Company began the day with an operation to clear the powerhouse that had eluded all attempts by Alpha Company. It was only when they scored a direct rocket launcher hit on the sub-station that the 13 EPCAF men holding it finally gave up. With that, the last pocket of resistance at Narsinghdi was eliminated.

Meanwhile, Mishra and Himmeth had assessed the situation, and both commanders again decided to exploit the situation and continue the dash for Dacca. Accordingly, Mishra ordered Himmeth to marshal his unit together and resume advance on Dacca as soon as possible.

Yet again, the guardsmen responded rapidly. By the time the remainder of 311 Mountain Brigade, including 65 Mountain Regiment, had been heli-landed across the Meghna, the battalion was ready and resumed its onward push to Dacca. Following closely behind was the rest of the brigade.

'We were feeling really kicked that Mishra had once again chosen our unit to lead the brigade advance,' Glucose beamed proudly.

At 1000 hours, on 12 December 1971, Alpha Company moved out in civil transport. The battalion HQ followed at 1300 hours. This time, however, they moved without Paunchy, who had been given yet another morphine shot to keep him happily sedated and then backloaded for treatment to Agartala.

The advance to Bulta, a small town on the east bank of Lakhiya river, about twelve kilometres short of Dacca, took place without any enemy interference. Noting the lack of enemy resistance, Mishra ordered 4 Guards to keep moving and push on to Barpa, another small town on the eastern banks of the Lakhiya river, a mere eight miles from Dacca; clearly, the end was near.

Operations were by now flowing so fast that it was becoming well nigh impossible to keep track of which Indian Army unit was where. If it was confusing on ground, it was becoming impossible for the Indian Air Force to identify friend and foe from the air.

Perhaps that is why, while advancing on Barpa with his company, Tuffy Marwah found himself under attack from the Indian Air Force. The strafing was pretty accurate, and they even managed to knock off the heel of his ammunition boot. Luckily, there were no other casualties.

Paunchy had, meanwhile, reached the ADS at Agartala, and was being treated for his wound. A Pakistani soldier, who had been shot in the ankle, occupied the bed next to him.

'While talking to him, I learnt that he was from 12 'Azad' Kashmir. He had been shot at the Arhand road block,' Paunchy said. He did not mention to him that it was his company that had been doing the shooting. 'It was pretty strange to be lying next to a guy whom one had been shooting at a couple of days ago,' said Paunchy with an inexplicable expression on his face. 'We spent one day together at the ADS. I learnt from him that he was very surprised and touched by the treatment being given to him by our forces.'

The Pakistani soldier told Paunchy that he had never expected to be treated so kindly. He had certainly never expected to be sharing a ward with an Indian Army officer, and being treated by the same doctors as an officer.

'Such a thing would never happen in our Army,' the soldier said, driving home the stark difference in two armies that had, until just a few years ago, marched under the same flag, been raised and trained together.

Back on the battlefield, by 2300 hours, 4 Guards had secured Barpa and had begun to dig in.

Barpa stands a mere eight miles from Dacca. In twelve short and bloody days, the Indian Army stood at the threshold of their final objective.

Morale in the Indian camp was soaring by now. Everyone sensed that the next couple of days would most probably be the most critical ones. Days that if properly handled would mean a successful end to the war.

Everyone was also aware that with their backs to the wall, the Pakistanis would now put up fierce resistance; they no longer had any more space to fall back upon.

All through the night, Himmeth went from company to company, meeting the men, rallying them, and getting them ready for the final push.

Not too far away from them, in the Pakistani camp at Dacca, the situation was exactly the opposite, and a grim fatal mood prevailed. The Pakistani Eastern Army Commander, General Niazi, had by now realized that the game was up, that he had been outwitted and outfought by the Indians.

'Niazi did not have much of a choice,' Shamsher Mehta pointed out. 'In addition to the fact that his forces were totally demoralized and no longer had the will to fight, he also had on his head the responsibility for the ten thousand odd Pakistani Army families that were presently in Dacca.'

Niazi knew that if he did not surrender to the Indian Army, and they happened to fall in the hands of the East Pakistanis, who were thirsting for vengeance, they would be lynched. The Bangladeshis would show them exactly the same mercy the Pakistani Army had shown them: none. This was amply clear from the fate of the few Pakistani soldiers who had the misfortune of falling in the hands of the locals. They would have been better off dead.

Sharply aware of the hatred his forces had fostered in the years preceding the war, Niazi contacted Yahya Khan and requested him to approach the UN for a ceasefire.

DAY THIRTEEN

13 DECEMBER 1971

Advance resumed well before first light of 13 December 1971. Alpha and Delta Companies, along with their Artillery OPs, moved astride the road from Barpa to Adamjee Jute Mills.

This road runs along, and almost parallel, to the hundred and fifty metre-wide Lakhiya river. Alpha Company, now commanded by Major G.M. Deboo, who had joined the battalion just two days ago, was moving astride the road, to the north of it. Delta Company was advancing on the south of the road.

Both companies hit the Lakhiya river and dug in along the river bank. Across the river, the Pakistanis were dug in and began to engage them with small arms' fire and artillery. It seemed the stalemate would continue for a while, since neither side could cross the river without certain, heavy losses.

Later that afternoon, a platoon of Charlie Company, supported by a section of mortars, moved to Bhiakar and tried to scare the enemy out of its position at Nagar Kachpur position.

'Marwah sahib especially chose to take me with him,' Sube Singh was unable to mask his pride. 'We gave supporting fire for his company several times. We were so effective that the Pakistanis soon called up their counter bombardment. And they were also good.'

When Pakistani artillery began raining down on them, one of the mortar men, Mokim Singh, took shelter in a brick kiln. Unfortunately, the brick kiln took a direct hit and simply disintegrated.

'We gathered his remains in a ground sheet,' Sube said somberly. 'Not that there was much left to gather. We didn't find a single piece bigger than this,' he held his hands up, about twelve inches apart, 'but whatever we did, we packed it up and sent it back.' Sube seemed to struggle for words. 'If it had not been for his tags, no one would have even known it was Mokim.'

The dog tags? Two metallic slivers with a number and name inscribed on them. In the end, that's all that remains of a soldier. That, and some memories... In the hearts of those who do not even get one last glimpse of his mortal remains.

I wondered briefly if anyone ever opened that ground sheet. Or had it simply been cremated along with the dozens of other bodies that were being ferried back by the administrative echelons.

Would it do anyone any good to have seen those shattered remains? Of what had once been a living, breathing man? Or was it better this way? To get back a pot of ashes in an earthen jar, with a red cloth tied across the mouth. And those inevitable dog tags, of course.

For a moment, I wanted to reach for my wallet and pull mine out. It had been years since I had shed the Olive Green uniform. Even longer since I had heard the soul-shattering roar of artillery fire, or the jarring clatter of guns fired; not in anger, but with the clinical precision of a surgeon ... by people trained in the art of war. But, despite the passage of years, my dog tags had remained in my wallet. As I knew they would till the very end. Shiny metallic reminders of the frail grasp we have on life.

The click of the tape recorder as it ran out intruded on the silence that had stalled in the room. That tiny metallic sound broke the severity of the moment.

'That engagement between Charlie Company and the Pakistani defenders at Nagar Kachpur lasted over three hours,' Tuffy spoke. He had been looking at me, as though waiting for me to be mentally present again. 'We did not manage to dislodge them then, but the hammering we gave them must have had the desired effect.'

Meanwhile back along the Lakhiya river, Granthi was mighty relieved when Himmeth called him to the battalion HQ and told him that his company would get rest that night.

Two weeks had elapsed since the first Indian combat boot had stepped across the International Border. Fourteen days and nights of non-stop movement, deep behind enemy lines, and in constant combat. With the Pakistanis on the run, morale was extremely high, but fatigue had set in very deeply and everyone could do with some sleep.

However, yet again, the Gods of War would deny them that sleep.

The Pakistani counter-attack on Alpha Company started just as Granthi's men were settling down for some rest.

The attack was well-planned, fiercely executed, and in full strength; as though the Pakistanis were aware that they were running out of options now and had to stop the Indians. It was a now or never kind of desperation.

Within minutes, Alpha was under pressure and the situation began to deteriorate fast.

Himmeth ordered Delta, being the closest, to reinforce Alpha Company.

Leaving behind some men to secure his location, Granthi moved fast and rushed to Alpha Company. Willy-nilly, the Pakistani attack was beaten back. However, the fight was far from over.

Unaware of the deployment of the Pakistani forces in and around Dacca, Himmeth had ordered two of the RCL guns to be deployed along the hundred and fifty metre wide Lakhiya river, and guard the crossing points to ensure no Pakistani troops could get across and cut off the battalion.

Lieutenant Colonel Himmeth Singh -- Deploying on the Lakhiya river

The RCL guns were placed under the command of one of the newly commissioned young officers posted with Alpha Company, who had joined the unit just a couple of months ago.

They had been in position for a while when a ferry filled with Pakistani soldiers began to nose its way across the river. Soon, the RCL guns were under fire. The JCO with the RCL detachment, thinking they were in danger of being encircled and cut off by the enemy, raised the alarm.

Who panicked and who didn't, remains a matter of conjecture. The fact remains that the Guardsmen abandoned the RCL guns and fell back towards the battalion position.

The Pakistanis spotted the opportunity and took over the guns' position. They did not bring the guns into use, but the position was invaluable as it allowed them to eyeball the deployment of 4 Guards. Within no time, they had deployed a Mortar OP who began to engage the Guardsmen, and inflicted thirty-three casualties.

Himmeth was furious when he came to know the RCL team team had withdrawn, leaving their guns behind.

'I had never seen him so angry. He simply lost it,' Glucose looked woebegone. 'He was furious with the young officer and the JCO. The Old Man not only scolded them, he also made it clear they would both be court-martialled for cowardice.'

'The JCO had almost twenty-three years of service then,' Jai Singh pointed out. 'He should have been more responsible, and should have given courage to the young officer, instead of panicking like that. But I guess such things happen in war.'

'The youngster was one of my company officers,' Paunchy intervened forcefully. 'I knew him very well, and he was no coward. He was a young lad, barely out of the Academy.'

'What happened was very unfortunate. I wish I had been there to support my boys. I would never have allowed the situation to develop the way it did. Unfortunately, I had been evacuated the previous day, and a company without its commander is like a rudderless boat,' CK looked angry with himself.

Meanwhile, Himmeth ordered Delta Company to clear the Pakistanis and recover their RCL guns.

By now, the Pakistanis were pretty well settled in and began to engage Granthi's men with direct fire, as well as artillery and mortars.

'One moment there was nothing, and the very next all hell had broken loose. We were under fire from all sides,' Granthi shook his head, perhaps still angry that he had not seen it coming.

The mortar fire was so effective that the Delta Company men were forced to seek cover. Unfortunately, several of them headed for the same culvert and took cover under it. It proved to be a fatal error, since the Pakistani OP was well-sited and had a grand view of the battlefield. The culvert took several direct hits due to which Delta took nineteen casualties. This was the biggest blow Delta Company had suffered till then. The irony was that it took place when victory was almost within reach.

The casualties would have been worse, had it not been for Lance Naik Dhuni Ram's heroic actions. Taking his section, he began to outflank the Pakistani position from the north. Though under constant and heavy mortar fire, Dhuni Ram completed his task and managed to make it hard for the Pakistanis to hold on to to the RCL position. But by the time the Pakistanis pulled back and the Guardsmen recovered the RCL guns, Dhuni Ram had been badly wounded and was evacuated shortly thereafter.

However, even then, a couple of the gun positions across the river were proving exceptionally irksome for Delta Company.

When Granthi shared this problem with Himmeth, he ordered Daljit to go forward to the Delta Company location and take care of the bunkers making life difficult for Granthi's men.

Daljit's day had not begun well. In fact, over the past few days, perhaps fuelled by the gunsmoke and dust, his asthma had begun to get worse. That Monday morning found him wheezing badly. Seeing his plight, Sutradhar advised his immediate evacuation.

However, Daljit was reluctant to go. He was aware that the battle for Dacca was almost on their heads now, and he would most certainly be needed.

The worried doctor and the reluctant patient were in the midst of their discussion when Himmeth's phone call came. It put an end to the discussion: at least for Daljit, it did.

Unmindful of the doctor's warning that he would soon be living up to his name—Shaheed meaning martyr—if he were not careful, Daljit headed for Delta Company. Breathing heavily, but steadfast in his resolve.

True to his form, he delivered yet another lethal airstrike on the Pakistani position across the river and silenced the more troublesome of their bunkers.

The rest of the night passed with sporadic bouts of gunfire and artillery shelling lighting up the dark skies.

Such was the sound and fury created by 4 Guards that General Niazi spoke to the Pakistani Commander-in-Chief General Hamid and asked him to request General Yahya Khan to expedite the ceasefire.

Yahya Khan is said to have replied, 'You have now reached a stage where further resistance is no longer humanly possible, nor will it serve any useful purpose. It will only lead to further loss of life and destruction. You should now take all necessary measures to stop fighting.'

It is certain that neither of the generals were aware that till then it was only 4 Guards and some elements of 311 Mountain Brigade and 65 Mountain Regiment that were knocking on the door to Dacca.

Brigadier Mishra, Himmeth and the Guardsmen – Victory is in sight

All this while, the Indian forces were being ferried across the Meghna—helicopters, an assortment of boats and ferries, everything they could lay their hands on was put to use.

Slowly but surely, the rest of the brigade started to build up on the 4 Guards' location.

DAY FOURTEEN

14 DECEMBER 1971

The morning of 14 December brought a team of the Western media, who sailed across the Lakhiya and arrived at the 4 Guards position toting a white flag. This lot was part of the effort that highlighted the massive atrocities committed by the Pakistani Army on the local population. They had also documented various war crimes committed by the Pakistanis on captured and wounded prisoners of war.

Himmeth with foreign correspondents

They also brought some good news. Apparently, shaken up by the battering they had received from Charlie Company the previous afternoon, the Pakistanis had abandoned the Nagar Kachpur position.

The Pakistanis had moved out in such a hurry that they even left behind a dead body, and, of course, a lot of stores and several tons of ammunition.

'By now, we had captured so much of their stuff that we were actually shelling the enemy with their own ammunition,' Maneck pointed out.

By that evening, Nagar Kachpur had been cleared and occupied by a platoon from Charlie Company. Soon, the rest of the company had also moved forward and had begun to build up on this platoon to properly secure Nagar Kachpur.

All this while, the rest of the Indian Army was also surging forward towards Dacca. Amongst the lot eager to move forward was Shamsher Mehta of 5 Armoured Squadron and his tanks. They had been with 4 Guards for so long that they were by now actually missing them, and were keen to catch up. Perhaps part of the incentive was the fact that Himmeth had promised Mehta a round of golf as soon as they captured Dacca!

Himmeth, Shammi Mehta and Glucose

Standing between Shamsher and 4 Guards was the mighty Meghna.

'Our PT 76's were amphibians, but they had basically been designed to cross European rivers, not make their way across rivers as wide as oceans, which is what the Meghna was.' Mehta, however, was not daunted.

The tank men decided they would use the tiny islands that dotted the river to get across. Thus began an interesting game of island hopping, where each tank would enter the river sufficiently upstream to allow the current to float it to the nearest island. From there to the next island, and then onwards to the next, till they finally made it across.

'It was a painstaking operation,' Mehta grinned, 'and at times also very scary, but we eventually managed to get all our tanks across.'

Soon, the tankmen were surging forward to link up with 4 Guards.

The Guardsmen, meanwhile, were busy wreaking some more psychological damage on to the beleaguered Pakistanis.

'By now, the 75/24 artillery guns had reached our location,' Glucose pointed it out on the makeshift map between us, which was a little more than a mess of scribbles. 'The 75/24 was a light mountain gun of Indian design. It could be dismantled and carried by mules, hence could get around, however the shells fired by these guns did not have much weight… they were only about seven pounds and lacked any significant destructive capability. However, we started shelling the Dacca cantonment.'

75mm Mtn. gun of 65 Mtn. Regt.The first salvo on Dacca 13th Dec.

To give the impression that they had a larger number of guns, the Indians would fire two-three rounds from each in quick succession. They may or may not have done much physical damage at the target end, but they certainly damaged the Pakistani morale.

The Mukti Bahini lends a helping hand. On the out skirts of Dacca.

Aware of the casualties that Delta Company had suffered the previous night, and also the fact that Alpha, too, had been in constant contact with the enemy, Himmeth now ordered Bravo Company to move forward and relieve them along the riverbank.

Handing over charge to Bravo Company, Granthi's boys were pulling out when the Pakistanis again engaged them with MMGs. However, this time, Bravo was ready and countered immediately.

In the brief but intense action that followed, three more Pakistanis lost their lives and Bravo captured one of the MMGs and two rifles of the Pakistani ambush party.

As the night of 14 December drew to a close, Charlie completed its move, and secured Nagar Kachpur.

By now, the brigade had also finished building up on the 4 Guards position and the Indian forces stood ready to take over Dacca and deliver the final blow to the Pakistanis.

DAY FIFTEEN

15 DECEMBER 1971

The dawn of 15 December saw Charlie Company take the battle to the main Pakistani position at the Adamjee Mills complex.

Charlie Company, along with a troop of tanks, attacked the enemy position on the east bank of Lakhya river and secured it by 1230 hours.

With a secure and firm base now available to him, Himmeth ordered his companies to start clearing the tiny pockets of Pakistanis holding out in the area. Delta was ordered to attack across the river and clear the opposite bank.

At the point at which they were deployed, the river was not too wide; perhaps two hundred and fifty feet. That was the good news. The bad news was that the Pakistani defenders on the opposite bank could bring down aimed fire on the guardsmen and even their 2-inch mortars were effective. Any attempt to cross the river within gun range would have meant a bloodbath and the Pakistani Army would have decimated the attackers. Another bad news was that the current was swift, therefore swimming across the river with full battle gear was not an option.

With that option not available, Granthi ordered his men to start looking for as many and whatever type of boats they could lay their hands on. Most of the boats had already been commandeered by the Pakistani Army and could be seen tied up in small lots across the river.

Search parties from Delta Company fanned out on both sides of the river, as the rest of the company got ready for the attack.

Just then, a couple of Pakistani soldiers emerged on the further bank. They were waving a makeshift white flag. It seemed like the war was over. However, the significance of the white flag took a while to register.

DAY SIXTEEN

16 DECEMBER 1971

'The Commandant was going around meeting the boys from Delta Company when the call came from the Brigade HQ. That's why I took the call. We came to know that the Pakistanis had surrendered,' Glucose beamed. 'What was even more thrilling was that our unit had been chosen to give a guard of honour to the Army Commander at 1600 hours that very day.'

The Adjutant immediately sent a radio message to all the company commanders that the Pakistanis had surrendered, and then ran to give the good news to Himmeth personally.

'At almost the same time as they were waving white flags, I got word from Glucose that the Pakistanis had surrendered.' Stepping up to the edge of the river, Granthi shouted to the Pakistanis to send across their boats. That triggered a mini-conference at the other end. Finally, some boats began to cross over to the Indian side.

'They may have surrendered, but they were still fully armed, and emotions were running high even then, or perhaps especially then. Surrender can never be a worthy option for any fighting man,' Granthi commented. 'Let me tell you, there were some very tense moments during the crossing.'

Eventually, the first elements of Delta Company landed on the other side.

In keeping with the lead-from-the-front tradition of the Indian Army, Granthi was in the first boat that crossed and the first to reach the Pakistani defences.

'It was quite funny,' Granthi grinned, 'because when I reached their location, I was dressed like a real *junglee*. I had not bathed for the last sixteen days,' he laughed, 'though it felt like much longer. And my uniform was totally torn. Can you imagine, I was wearing trousers I had taken from a dead Pakistani and boots from another! Even those were in tatters. And on top was my Indian Army shirt, which was really ragged.'

I tried to imagine him stepping out of the boat dressed like that. It was a hard sell.

In stark contrast, the Pakistani officer who came up to greet the first boatload of Indian troops was in full ceremonial dress, a medley of shining brass and gold. So confident had the Pakistani High Command been (of emerging victorious over the Indians), that all their officers had carried their ceremonial uniforms with them in battle.

'Perhaps, if they had brought their fighting spirit along, it may have held them in better stead.' That comment came from a corner of the room.

'Hand over your pistol,' Granthi told the officer, 'and tell your men to get all their weapons and deposit them here in one lot.'

'Who the hell are you?' the Pakistani officer retorted rudely. 'I will only talk to your officer.'

'I am the Company Commander, my friend,' Granthi replied evenly, aware that he was quite a sight to look at.

One of the Pakistani JCOs came up and accosted Granthi, 'Oye! Don't you dare speak to my sahib like that.' He admonished in Punjabi, 'Get your Company Commander here.'

'I am the Company Commander,' Granthi repeated again, more firmly this time.

Then the rest of the guardsmen surged around their Company Commander and their behaviour made the fact too obvious too ignore.

The Pakistani officer appeared stunned as he quietly removed his weapon and handed it over to Granthi.

That look on the Pakistani JCO's face remained long after they had gone through the surrender formalities, of which there were not many.

Finally, unable to stop himself any longer, the Pakistani JCO came up to Granthi and said, 'You know sahib, your officers and our men, we can win any war together.' There were tears in his eyes as he spoke. His tone was low, as though voicing that thought was some kind of betrayal.

'But that was what most of the Pakistani soldiers felt about their officers,' Granthi's eyes, too, were strangely moist. 'I remember, even at one of their BOPs (Border Out Post), when we had been about to attack, their company commander left the post and returned to the rear. We heard the exchange of words he had with his platoon JCO over the radio. His JCO openly told him that even when he (the officer) had said he was going back to get reinforcements, all of them had known he would not come back to face the Indian attack.'

There was a long pause as we all mulled over that. Every man present in the room had worn the Olive Green, had led men into battle. Not one had any ambiguity that commanders do not leave their men alone to face the music. This was the code, a very basic code, which all warriors live by. And die for.

We could all empathize with the Pakistani JCO; the very fact that he had so openly voiced this feeling to an outsider, and an enemy no less, was a clear indication of how deep the rot had run into their officer cadre, and how dark the resentment in their rank and file.

I said nothing. There was nothing to say, really.

Himmeth was obviously thrilled when he got orders that 4 Guards would be giving a guard of honour to the Army Commander at Dacca. It was as though all the blood and sweat spilt by his men in the past sixteen days had been vindicated. He ordered Tuffy Marwah to lead the Guard of Honour.

Frantic activity broke out in the battalion, as the guardsmen got ready to rush to Dacca.

It was already past noon and time was short. They had a river to cross, eight miles to cover, and a parade to prepare for. The switch from battle mode to ceremonial mode is not easy, even in the best of times. Doing so after sixteen days of non-stop battle, with virtually no notice and right when they were in the thick of executing an attack, was infinitely harder.

Also, the Pakistanis were not in an exceptionally co-operative mood. Despite the truce having been declared by the Pakistani Eastern Army Commander, General A.A.K. Niazi, some of the the lower ranks and the isolated pockets of troops who had yet not received the orders to surrender, kept fighting. All Indian attempts to reach out with the white flag were also rebuffed initially.

Finally, either the sustained pressure, or fresh orders from their bosses, got to them, because they were asked to surrender. However, it did not seem like the gods wanted the guardsmen to be a part of the parade.

As soon as the guardsmen crossed the river, thousands of Bengalis surrounded them. Though the Pakistani Army had been unable to stop the sweeping tide of the Indian Army, the Bangaldeshis certainly did.

'Moving even an inch in any direction was impossible,' Glucose gave a rueful smile. 'They were all over us, and the mood of the crowd was so boisterous and euphoric,' he broke off. Finally, after a very long pause, 'It is hard to explain what everyone was feeling.'

His choked voice and moist eyes communicated that to me far more easily than any words could have.

With the guardsmen out of the running, it was finally the Pakistani troops who gave the ceremonial parade. Perhaps beffitingly so, the monster that had tortured and tormented the populace for so long was finally kneeling before it.

Glocuse handed me some photographs of the parade.

One person who was unable to enjoy or participate in the victory celebrations was Daljit Singh Shaheed.

The brave, young pilot collapsed within hours of reaching Dacca, and was hospitalized in a very acute condition.

So commendable had been his performance throughout those sixteen days that Himmeth had no hesitation in recommending him for the Vir Chakra; despite being one of the youngest Forward Air Controllers he had not only brought down very effective air strikes on the enemy, but often volunteered to accompany patrols into enemy territory. For his stellar role in the war Shaheed was awarded the Vayu Sena Medal.

With the flurry of surrender ceremonies behind them, one of the first things that Himmeth did was to take a round of all the places where the Pakistanis were holding Indian prisoners of war, at least the few that they had not summarily executed.

The Jagganath Hostel, which used to house the Hindu students of Dacca University, was one such place. The Dacca University had been a focal point for the development of the East Pakistan freedom movement and as such drawn the ire of the Pakistani top brass. In March 1971, on the orders of General Yahya Khan and Zulfikar Ali Bhutto, the Pakistani armed forces had launched 'Operation Searchlight' to destroy this freedom movement. Armed with heavy weapons and accompanied by tanks, three task forces had encircled the university on 25 March 1971; Unit 41 from the east, Unit 88 from the south and Unit 26 from the north. Jagganath hostel had drawn special attention of the attacking forces since it housed Hindu students; hundreds of them were massacred.

Guardsman Suresh Singh, of Number Three Platoon, Alpha Company, had been taken into Pakistani captivity on 2 December 1971. Though badly wounded, he had received little medical treatment and even less food in the past two weeks. He and other prisoners were stuffed in filthy rooms, which were never cleaned.

'In fact the first time a doctor even came to see us was only on 15 December 1971,' Suresh explained. 'That day, they had the rooms cleaned and also gave us food. We all got worried thinking they were going to kill us after this last meal.'

When Suresh saw Himmeth walk into the prison, he thought their Commandant had also been taken prisoner and was dismayed.

Guardsman Suresh Singh

'Then I saw the same doctor who had come to see us the previous day come scurrying up to Colonel Himmeth and say, "I have looked after your men really well, sir." But Commandant sahib just ignored him. He came straight up and hugged all of us one by one. He then told us to gather all the 4 Guards boys in the prison. That is when we realized that the Pakistanis had surrendered. Soon, we were all crying with happiness.'

Suresh had been one of the Alpha Company boys who had been captured during the fateful Pakistani counter-attack on Desraj's platoon at the smaller bridge at Kodda on 2nd December. He had witnessed every second of that bloody battle.

'Our platoon, alongwith an Artillery OP officer Captain M.P. Singh, was ordered by Major Chandrakant to deploy on the smaller bridge on the railway line between Akhaura and Brahmanbaria, while he moved ahead with the rest of the company to capture the railway station at Kodda. We had started digging foxholes when we saw a railway engine and two or three bogies coming towards our position from Kodda railway station. We knew there were Pakistanis in them and started digging faster so that we would be able to defend the position. However, it was worrying, since our platoon was taking up position on both sides of the railway track and the wagons coming towards us would split apart our defences.' Using a stick, Suresh drew a rough diagram on the ground.

And then continued: 'Just then, we also saw some tanks coming towards us. That brought a lot of relief since we thought they were our tanks. We knew our tanks had gotten stuck the previous night on the other side of the Titas river, but assumed they had managed to cross over somewhow. To our horror, the tanks began firing at us. That totally confused us, and even now we did not return fire thinking they had made a mistake. By now, the wagons had also stopped in the middle of our position, dividing us in two, and they also opened fire. Many of our men were killed, and many more wounded. Then to add to our problems, some Pakistani infantry also attacked us. By now, we also started fighting back. I saw my section commander Naik Ram Khilawan run up to a tank and toss a grenade inside. He even pulled out a Pakistani soldier and hit him, but by then the others attacked him and he went down. I could see he was badly wounded, but the Pakistanis didn't show any mercy. They poured diesel on him and burnt him alive. It was such a cruel and cowardly thing to do.'

Suresh's expression made it evident that despite the passage of years, the horror was still fresh in his mind.

'Badly wounded by now, the three of us, Lance Naik Pirabhu Ram, Guardsman Giranth Singh and myself, were taken prisoners. Before my eyes, the Pakistanis shot Pirabhu and Giranth. I asked them why they were doing this when we had surrendered, but that made no difference to them and they shot a couple of other men, too. However, for some reason, perhaps thinking that I was badly wounded and would die soon anyway, they did not shoot at me again. Lying outside my foxhole, I saw them use their tanks to crush Lakpath Singh and Topo. That is when I fainted.'

From the expressions visible on the faces around, it was obvious I was not the only one having trouble reconciling with such bestial behaviour from soldiers. One of the men in the room said angrily, 'What's surprising? These Pakistanis were animals then and are animals now. They tortured and mutilated the bodies of our soldiers in Kargil and still go around beheading people. Nothing has changed.' Suresh resumed his narrative.

'When I recovered, there were many Pakistani soldiers, including some officers, looking at us. I was picked up along with some other wounded people and shoved into a truck and moved from there. It was a horrid journey. We were given neither adequate food nor any medical treatment. They rushed us away by trucks and boats and a week later, we arrived in Dacca. And that's where we remained till Commandant sahib walked in to rescue us.'

Suresh was one of the seven guardsmen picked up from that camp by Himmeth. These were the lucky seven, still alive, since General Niazi had asked for the 4 Guards boys to be brought to Dacca for interrogation. However, that had proved to be the only saving grace for them.

'I was put on a stretcher and taken along with the other prisoners to the battalion headquarters, from where we were sent by helicopter to Agartala. After two surgeries, I was transferred first to Guwahati and then to Delhi. That is where, after all these months, I met my family.'

The damage caused to Suresh, as well as many others, by the refusal of the Pakistanis to render any medical aid, was horrendous. In Suresh's case, his wounds had turned gangreneous. It was only after months of hospitalization and several surgeries that some of them finally made it back to the unit. Many others were invalided out.

Himmeth returned to the battalion with his seven battered, but happy, men when he found a message from General Niazi waiting for him.

'The Pakistani General was originally commissioned in 1 Rajput, which is what we were before we became 4 Guards,' Glucose explained. 'He had learnt from one of our men who had been captured by the Pakistanis during the battle of Akhaura, that our battalion was leading the charge on Dacca.'

The General was keen to meet Himmeth. However, Himmeth was not. He politely declined the invitation.

'Himmeth told me that he would never go to meet an officer who had condoned so much cruelty and bestiality by the men under his command,' Glucose explained. 'Things like this, which were unbecoming of an officer, a soldier, were anathema to Himmeth.'

I leaned back in my chair.

What better end can there be to a story about a war?

Times will change. Civilizations will rise and fall. And men, being men, wars will be fought, lost and won.

But men like Himmeth lend some semblance of sanity, respect, and dignity to even such a terrible thing as war.

It was as though Glucose had heard my thoughts. 'Himmeth was Himmeth,' he summed up.

It was a while before I could move again. Eventually, reaching out, I shut down the recording machine.

My march down this bloody road had ended.

DEATH OF A WAR & BIRTH OF A NATION

The 17th of December saw East Pakistan caught in the throes of delirious celebration.

Mishra – mobbed by jubiliant Bangladeshis

More than anywhere else, the streets of Dacca were choked with celebrating masses. It was hard to tell that just hours ago, war had ravaged this country.

4 Guards at General Maneckshaw's *darbar* in Dacca – after a well-fought war

Participating in these festivities, albeit far more quietly, were Brigadier Mishra, Commander 311 Mountain Brigade, Colonel Himmeth and Major Shamsher Mehta (the Armoured Squadron Commander). They finally did play the long promised round of golf at the Services Gymkhana Club in Dacca.

The club, inaugurated in 1966 by the Pakistani dictator General Yahya Khan, had once hosted what they thought was the pride of the Pakistani Army.

That day, what it hosted was certainly the pride of the Indian Army.

Sam Bahadur with Himmeth and other officers of 311 Mountain Brigade

A few days later, word filtered down that Sheikh Mujib-ur-Rehman was returning to Dacca. He was finally being released from prison and coming back to Dacca via Delhi and Calcutta in a Caribou aircraft or a helicopter belonging to the Indian Air Force.

4 Guards was given the task of providing protection to him at the Dacca airfield. However, his arrival kept getting delayed. Finally, news filtered down that he had been flown by the Pakistanis to London, and so would come from there in a British RAF Comet 4 aircraft.

The runway of Dacca airport had been heavily bombed and cratered by the Indian Air Force at the outbreak of the war, and had still not been repaired. The pilot flew over the damaged runway a couple of times before he finally managed to land. It must have been a hair-raising landing, as the pilot barely managed to bring the aircraft to a halt a few metres short of the first crater.

'I had not heard a louder roar in my life,' Paunchy, who, though still not fully healed, had been unable to keep himself away from Dacca and was now watching the action from the control tower. 'When Mujib emerged from the aircraft, it was as though the world had gone mad. There were thousands of Bengalis at the airfield and they gave voice to their pleasure when they saw the man who had spearheaded their struggle for freedom.'

Paunchy was unable to contain himself and despite orders to the contrary, rushed forward to shake hands with Mujib-ur-Rehman.

Soon, it was time to bid farewell to the land they had shed blood on and wrested freedom for. On 12 March 1972, as a befitting acknowledgement of the battalion's role in the war, 4 Guards was selected to represent the Indian Army at a farewell parade held at Dacca stadium.

4 Guards marching past – Farewell parade at Dacca Stadium on 12 March 1972

Thousands of jubiliant Bengalis packed the stadium, more vociferous and excitable than ever before.

Sheikh Mujib addresses the parade and thanks India

The parade was commanded by Lieutenant Colonel Himmeth Singh, and reviewed personally by Sheikh Mujib-ur-Rehman. The Sheikh addressed our troops and thanked the Government of India and the Indian Army for their help and sacrifices in the liberation of his country.

Sheikh Mujib signing the 4 Guards Visitor Book
Major Kharbanda, Major General J.F.R. Jacob, Lieutenant General Jagjit Singh Aurora and Sheikh Mujib-ur-Rehman

THE HOMECOMING

A young battalion comprising really young officers had gone to war. The youngest was nineteen-year-old Medappa. In the real world, he would have just stopped wearing braces and barely have been given a driver's license. In this gory world, he found himself leading thirty-eight men (two for every year of his life) through a nightmare of mud, slush, machine gun fire and artillery shelling. Paunchy, the second-in-command, was twenty-eight, and in between them lay the other fourteen officers. Himmeth, who commanded this motley group, was forty-three, twenty-one years of which had been spent in uniform.

Officers and JCOs of 4 Guards

Seated (L-R): Major S. Marwah, Panditjee, Major Gus Debu, S. M. Man Singh, Lieutenant Colonel Himmeth Singh, Lieutenant Colonel K.M. Muthanna, Subedar Rawat Singh, Major Chandra Kant, JCO Dogra.

Standing (L-R): Subedar Gurvachan Singh, Ramji Lal, Raghubir, --------, Lieutenants Yadav and Jaiveer with the regimental colours, Captain V. K. Dewan, Tibat Singh, Ramlochan, Naib Subedar Basti Ram.

Standing last row (L-R): Bishan Singh, Kashmir Singh, Dhuri Ram,--------, Subedar Makhan Lal, Tirath Singh, Desram, Edu. JCO, Naib Subedar Subhash Chander.

In the aftermath, like the slowly fading rush of adrenaline, came the reality of what we call normal life. The change was surreal; perhaps completely unreal. Each one of the men handled it differently. Some felt there was nothing else the Army could offer them, and left. Some shed the uniform, feeling hurt and betrayed, by a nation that chose to forget them. Some, career-oriented soldiers who could not envisage a life less ordinary, stayed on.

Himmeth Singh rose through the ranks till he became a Lieutnant General and was awarded the PVSM (Param Vishisth Seva Medal). He served as GOC 10 Corps, Commandant IMA, and Commandant NDC, after which he retired on 30 June 1987. Post retirement, he served as advisor to His Excellency, Sheikh Hamad bin Khalifa Al Thani, the then Defence Minister and now the Emir of Qatar. Himmeth passed away on 3 January 2000.

Himmeth bids farewell to fellow officers

Paunchy (Major Chandrakant), who was awarded the Vir Chakra for his role in this war, and Tuffy (Major S. P. Marwah), the Sena Medal, both took premature retirement and are now self employed.

Major V. K. Dewan received a 'Mention in Dispatches', served his full term in the Army and is now self employed.

Major Kharbanda, also awarded the Vir Chakra, stayed on in service till his retirement as a Lieutnant Colonel. He expired soon after, on 18 April 1998.

Granthi (Lieutenant Colonel Surinder Singh) and Lieutenant Colonel K. S. Yadav, both commanded 4 Guards eventually, and after retirement are now self employed.

"The ones that nation forget--widows & veterans."

Front row: Honorary Captain Pati Ram, Pushpa Devi, W/o.Giranth Singh, Shanti Devi W/o.Hans Ram, Guardsman Brij Nandan, Guardsman Ramnath, ---------.

Second row: Naik Shri Kishan, Guardsman Subedar, Guardsman Ujagar Lal, Guardsman Ram Sarthi,--------, Guardsman Suresh Singh, Guardsman Ramdin, Guardsman Ram Saran.

Third row: Guardsman Ram Prakash, Guardsman Jiva Lal, Major Chandrakant VrC., Guardsman Raghubir Singh, Guardsman Salik Ram, -------

Major L. M. Singh, Lieutenant Colonel Amar Singh Chauhan, Lieutenant Colonel B. B. Midha, Lieutenant S. Karmarkar, Captain Sahani, Major Vijay Uppal and Brigadier Medappa also completed their Army tenures, and are now self employed.

Captain RAK' Maneck retired as a Lieutnant Colonel and is now the regional head of Maharashtra, Gujarat and Goa, of the

Mumbai-based Securitrans India Private Limited, a cash-in-transit company.

Lieutnant General Shamsher Mehta (Armoured Corps), PVSM, AVSM and Bar, VSM, retired after serving as GOC-in-C (General Officer Commanding in Chief) Western Command, and is now settled in Pune.

Major Rajendra Mohan (Armoured Corps) took voluntary retirement and once he had recovered from his horrific burn wounds, served as an Executive Director with ONGC (Oil and Natural Gas Corporation Limited).

Of the JCOs, NCOs and Other Ranks, I wish I could give a detailed listing of each one of them, since they were heroes, each one of them. And have been forgotten by the country, as soldiers are wont to be.

However, I do not think this story would be complete without mentioning at least a few of them, and their widows.

It was the near fanatic dedication of Mrs Jane Himmeth Singh that brought to light the stories of the veterans of this war and their widows, who would have been well nigh impossible to find otherwise. But I am glad they were found and I can share these stories with you. It will help you realize the plight of the loved ones of those who gave their lives for the country.

Bhind and Morena, in the badlands of the Chambal ravines, are one of the traditional recruitment areas for the Guards regiment. The hundred-kilometre ride to the Bhind Sainik Kalyan Board, on a dusty, bumpy road, took almost five hours.

Another half-an-hour's drive through the narrow lanes of Bhind brings one to the Shaheed (Martyr's) Colony, built by the government for war widows of the Indian Army. Contrary to the grand name, the colony is just a cluster of terribly dilapidated huts, not very different from the slums in Delhi, however without the TV antennae or any other signs of modernity or prosperity.

Navigating past unplastered and unfinished red brick houses, narrow unpaved lanes, and uncovered drains finally led us to the house of Kailashi, the widow of Guardsman Jagdish Prasad.

Kailashi was sixteen when she received the telegram informing her of her husband's death. She was living with her in-laws and had been married only a few months earlier, when Jagdish had come on leave. That was the first and the last time she saw him. She does not remember what he looked like for she had no photograph of his. In due course, she was informed that she was entitled to a special family pension of 132 rupees per month, which would continue only till the time she did not marry again, unless she married the brother of Jagdish.

Pushpa Devi, widow of Guardsman Giranth Singh

Kailashi, widow of Guardsman Jagdish Prasad, with Mrs. Jane Himmeth Singh

Next to the house of Kailashi is the house of Lakhpath Singh of Alpha Company, who, whilst wounded at Kodda, had been deliberately run over by a Pakistani tank. Lakhpath's wife was eighteen on the day he died. And she was pregnant then. Shortly after giving birth, she passed away, leaving the boy to be brought up by his grandparents.

Not much further away from them, in Fatehgarh district, lives Pushpa Devi, the widow of Guardsmen Giranth Singh. She was married to him when she was all of thirteen years old, and he, a grand sixteen. One year later, she joined him at his home, and in the five years that followed, bore him two sons and a daughter.

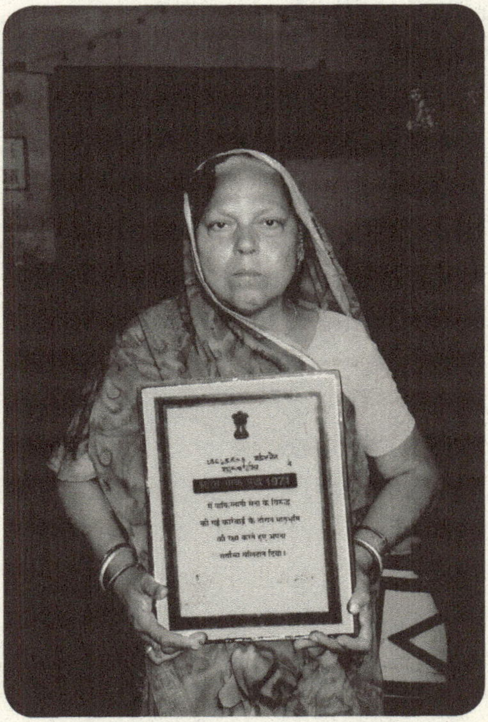

Madhuri Dixit, widow of Guardsman Raghunath Dixit

Giranth enlisted when he was twenty, and soon joined the proud ranks of 4 Guards. A few months before war broke out, Giranth arrived for two months' leave. It was during this leave that their fourth child was conceived. A child who would never see his father, since Giranth Singh was declared 'Missing In Action' during the war. The loss of her husband netted Pushpa

Devi the handsome amount of forty-two rupees per month. This was what she was expected to bring up her family of five on.

Several years elapsed before she was informed that Giranth had been killed and she was now officially a widow. From twenty-six years of age, Pushpa Devi has soldiered on, bringing up four children, two of them blind, on a meagre pension of 132 rupees a month.

Somewhat better off than them is Madhuri Dixit, the wife of Guardsman Raghunath Dixit.

To reach Madhuri's small, but *pucca* house, one has to enter deep into the heart of Farrukhabad town and jump over open sewers and garbage heaps. She was all of seventeen years old when she got word that her husband was no more. Today, all she has of him is a photograph taken from his paybook, enlarged and morphed to include her standing beside him in her bridal finery. That, and some hazy memories, perhaps as hazy as the nation's memories of its men in uniform, who sacrifice their lives in each war.

BACK TO THE PRESENT

Naik Ganesha Singh

'I never thought I would see you again, sahib,' Naik Ganesha Singh's voice cracked as the wizened old man reached out to embrace Paunchy. The babel of voices and excited expressions on the faces of the others conveyed the same sentiment.

I stood beside Mrs. Jane, Himmeth's wife, watching them. They had gathered at Fatehgarh, to meet us and tell their story, rallied together by the call of the officers they had followed into battle all those years ago. I could see they were eager to tell their stories. Many had forgotten most of the stories. The others, who remembered, had given up hope that their stories would ever be told.

Age and life had taken its toll on them, but it was easy to see that they still retained that spark, that very special spark, which separates heroes from mere mortals.

I have had the pleasure of meeting war veterans before, and it was not hard for me to understand what they would have been like, back in those days.

Lord Tennyson's ode to Ulyssses swept through me, unbidden:

Though much is taken, much abides; and though
We are not now that strength which in old days
Moved earth and heaven; that which we are, we are;
One equal temper of heroic hearts,
Made weak by time and fate, but strong in will
To strive, to seek, to find, and not to yield.

I sat with them till the sun was low over the horizon, and heard their half-forgotten, half-scrambled stories. And these are what I have put together for you in the story I just shared.

Suresh Singh, Ganesha Singh, Mukund Singh, Tirath Singh and Pushpa Devi: forgotten remanants of a forgotten war.

As I walked away, I could not help think… With pride for what they had accomplished, with grief for all that they had lost, and with shame at the nation that had forgotten them. These simple, yet brave, men who had wrested freedom for a people not their own.

Despite everything, I had the satisfaction of knowing that the Garud they had marched under would be proud of them.

Letters of Appreciation received by 4 Guards

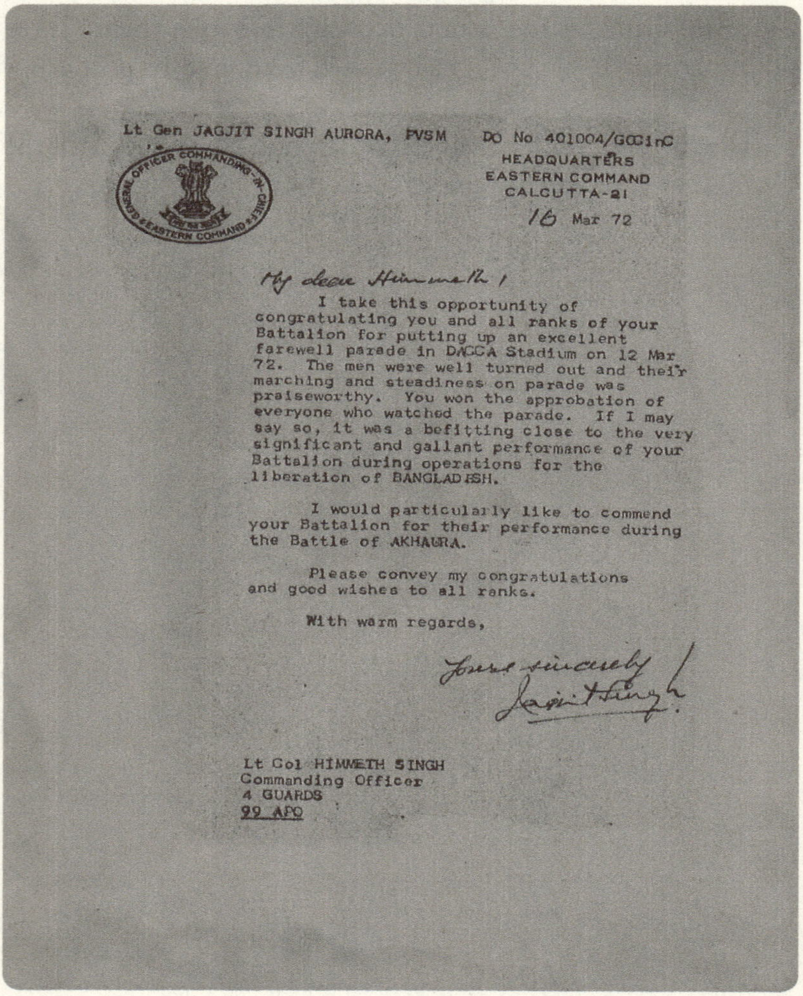

Lt Gen JAGJIT SINGH AURORA, PVSM

DO No 401004/GOCinC
HEADQUARTERS
EASTERN COMMAND
CALCUTTA-21

16 Mar 72

My dear Himmeth,

I take this opportunity of congratulating you and all ranks of your Battalion for putting up an excellent farewell parade in DACCA Stadium on 12 Mar 72. The men were well turned out and their marching and steadiness on parade was praiseworthy. You won the approbation of everyone who watched the parade. If I may say so, it was a befitting close to the very significant and gallant performance of your Battalion during operations for the liberation of BANGLADESH.

I would particularly like to commend your Battalion for their performance during the Battle of AKHAURA.

Please convey my congratulations and good wishes to all ranks.

With warm regards,

Yours sincerely,
Jagjit Singh

Lt Col HIMMETH SINGH
Commanding Officer
4 GUARDS
99 APO

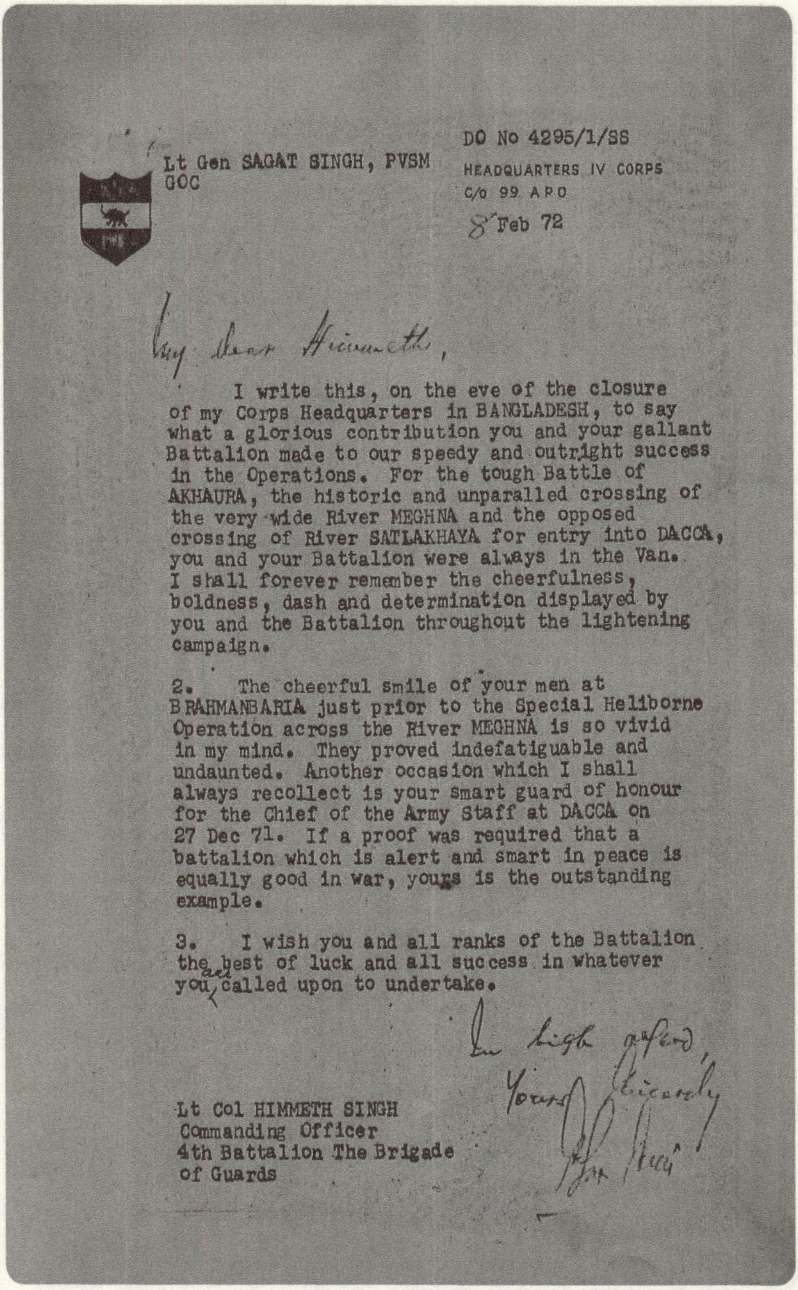

DO No 4295/1/SS

Lt Gen SAGAT SINGH, PVSM
GOC

HEADQUARTERS IV CORPS
C/o 99 APO

8 Feb 72

My dear Himmeth,

I write this, on the eve of the closure of my Corps Headquarters in BANGLADESH, to say what a glorious contribution you and your gallant Battalion made to our speedy and outright success in the Operations. For the tough Battle of AKHAURA, the historic and unparalled crossing of the very wide River MEGHNA and the opposed crossing of River SATLAKHAYA for entry into DACCA, you and your Battalion were always in the Van. I shall forever remember the cheerfulness, boldness, dash and determination displayed by you and the Battalion throughout the lightening campaign.

2. The cheerful smile of your men at BRAHMANBARIA just prior to the Special Heliborne Operation across the River MEGHNA is so vivid in my mind. They proved indefatiguable and undaunted. Another occasion which I shall always recollect is your smart guard of honour for the Chief of the Army Staff at DACCA on 27 Dec 71. If a proof was required that a battalion which is alert and smart in peace is equally good in war, yours is the outstanding example.

3. I wish you and all ranks of the Battalion the best of luck and all success in whatever you are called upon to undertake.

In high regard,
Yours sincerely,

Lt Col HIMMETH SINGH
Commanding Officer
4th Battalion The Brigade
of Guards

From:-Maj Gen BF GONSALVES, PVSM
Chief of Staff

DO No 1884/2/GEN
HEADQUARTERS II CORPS
C/O 56 APO
12 Mar 73

My dear Himmet

As you are aware, one year ago today 4 GUARDS paraded before Seikh Mujibar Rehman at the Dacca Stadium on the eve of the departure of the Indian Army from Bangladesh. It bears repetition to state again that it was a most splended and spectacular parade; it made one proud of being an Indian, and the cheers of the Dacca crowd still ring in my ears. However, that is not the reason for this letter : it is that it has just occurred to me that I have not sufficiently recognised the magnificent contribution made by the Battalion towards the successful conduct of the operations leading to the fall of Dacca.

2. The performance of the Battalion throughout the war, and in the months preceding it, was of the highest order. Nevertheless, the Battle of Akhaura was undoubtedly your greatest moment. The details of the battle are all there for the historians to study; but the indomitable spirit of your Battalion was what contributed most to Victory and it is that spirit and rock-like steadfastness which I saw your Battalion display that I today salute. In the field of tactics it is the encircling movement which manoeuvred the enemy out of the formidable defences of Akhaura. You will no doubt recall that there were some doubting Thomases who felt that such a major encircling movement, involving the crossing of a wide water course, all in the course of one night, was not a feasible preposition. The "First Rajputs"

...2/-

-2-

DO No
HEADQUARTERS II CORPS
C/O APO

certainly surprised everyone, including ofcourse the enemy, by their swift and intrepid move across country, to establish the block in the rear; thereby contributing so greatly to the enemy's discomfiture. The subsequent skirmishing, involving hand-to-hand encounters with the Pakistani infantrymen and close encounters with his tanks, finally forced the enemy to flee.

3. Thereafter, the pursuit of the enemy to the gates of Dacca saw your Battalion once again in the van. The heli-borne assault across the mighty Meghna River was yet another feather in the Battalion's cap. I remember how your Battalion was still locked in combat with the enemy before Ashuganj when it was decided to launch the heli-borne assault. How you managed to successfully disengage, plan and launch the operation in the short space of twenty-four hours will remain a military mystery. The contribution of this assault to final victory was incalculable. When the course of operations is analysed, I have no doubt that it will be shown that your assault across the Meghna, which was the first incursion into what has come to be called the 'Dacca Bowl', was the signal for the general withdrawal of the enemy on all fronts.

4. I have discoursed at some length on your Battalion's actions, because as your erstwhile Divisional Commander I feel that your unit's contribution to final victory has not been fully

...3/-

-3-

DO No
HEADQUARTERS II CORPS
C/O APO

recognised. I hope that this will set the record right, atleast as between the heroic"First Rajputs" and their Divisional Commander of old. Pray tell the officers and men that I once again salute their courage and steadfastness in battle.

With very best wishes,

Yours sincerely,

Brigadier HIMMET SINGH
Commander
67 Infantry Brigade
C/O 56 APO

Brigadier RN MISRA VrC
Commander

DO No 2489/G(Ops)27
HQ 311 MTN BDE
C/O. 99 APO
21 Dec 71

My dear Himmeth,

With triumphant entry of 4 GUARDS(1 RAJPUT) into DACCA on 16 Dec, the war has come to an end with total victory over the enemy. The achievements of your Battalion have been exemplary and in keeping with your glorious past. I am sure history will reflect your these operations in glowing words.

2. The infiltration of your Battalion over an extremely difficult terrain, under the very nose of the enemy, with lightening speed is praise worthy. It was determination and tanacity of both the leaders and the lead that the infiltration; inspite of delay in completion of phase one of the Brigade plan, was completely successful. The Battalion had to negotiate marshy area and wade through chest deep back-waters of river TITAS. Establishing the Battalion at KODDA, SHYAMNAGAR and BARISAL, at places only 200 yards from enemy position and digging down before day-break was an achievement of which I do not know of a parallel. Determined fight against armour and infantry attack put up by Majors CHANDRA KANT and KHARBANDA has earned every-one's admiration.

3. The ambush laid by your Battalion on road KASBA - BRAHMAN BARIA on 6 Dec achieved complete surprise and took a heavy toll of the enemy. It enabled speedy entry of our forces in BRAMAN BARIA.

4. The speed with which, inspite of administrative difficulties, your Battalion, at four hours notice was ready for Heliborne operation on 9 Dec has earned the admination of both GOCs 57 Mtn Div and IV Corps. They have asked me to convey their congratulations to you and your Battalion.

......2/-

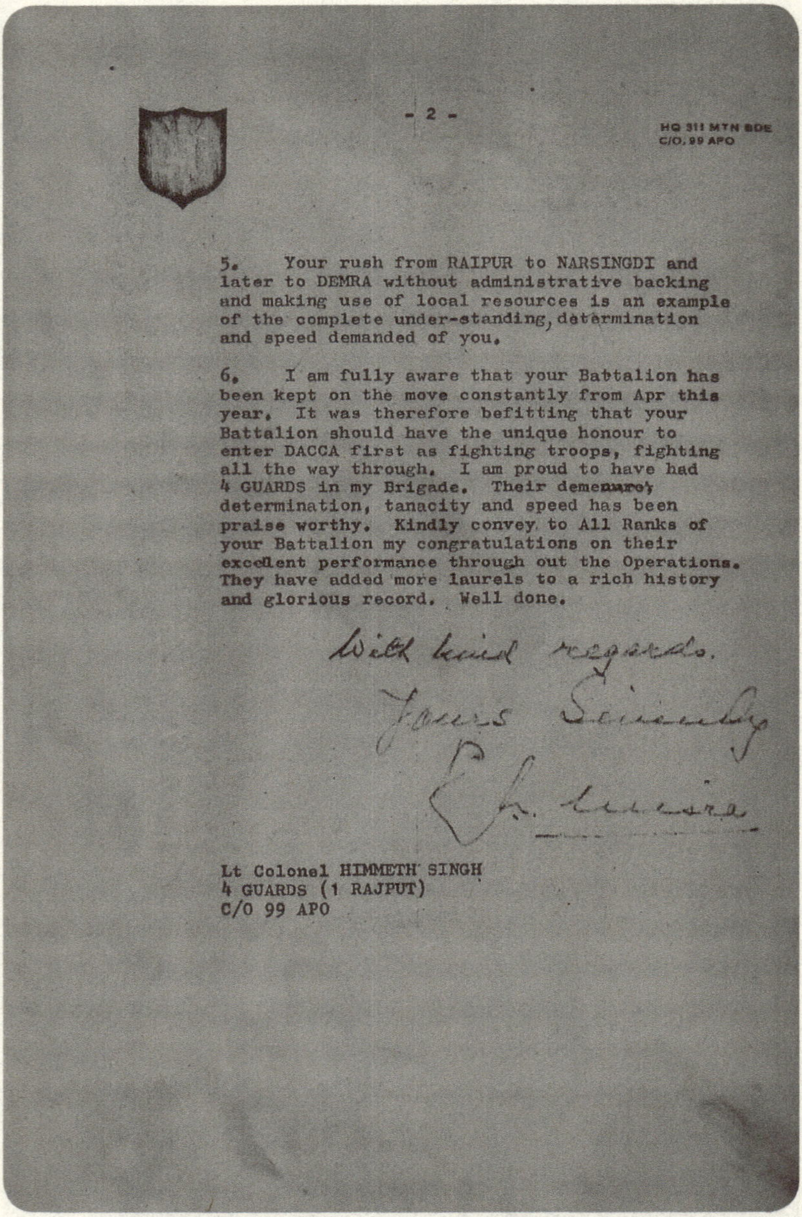

- 2 -

HQ 311 MTN BDE
C/O, 99 APO

5. Your rush from RAIPUR to NARSINGDI and later to DEMRA without administrative backing and making use of local resources is an example of the complete under-standing, determination and speed demanded of you.

6. I am fully aware that your Battalion has been kept on the move constantly from Apr this year. It was therefore befitting that your Battalion should have the unique honour to enter DACCA first as fighting troops, fighting all the way through. I am proud to have had 4 GUARDS in my Brigade. Their demeanure, determination, tanacity and speed has been praise worthy. Kindly convey to All Ranks of your Battalion my congratulations on their excellent performance through out the Operations. They have added more laurels to a rich history and glorious record. Well done.

With kind regards.

Yours Sincerely

[illegible]

Lt Colonel HIMMETH SINGH
4 GUARDS (1 RAJPUT)
C/O 99 APO

Officers of 4 Guards Who Fought the 1971 War

1. Lieutenant Colonel Himmeth Singh, Commandant
2. Major V. Uppal, D Company Commander
3. Major Chandra Kant, Vir Chakra, A Company Commander
4. Major S.P. Marwah, Sena Medal, C Company Commander
5. Major I.P. Kharbanda, Vir Chakra, B Company Commander
6. Major A.S. Chouhan, Adm Company Commander
7. Major V.K. Dewan, Adjutant
8. Captain Surinder Singh, D Company Commander (with effect 1 Dec 1971)
9. Lieutenant Ram Raj Singh, RCL PIatoon Commander
10. Captain L.M. Singh, Company Officer
11. Captain S.S. Sahni, B Company Commander (with effect 9 Dec 1971)
12. 2nd Lieutenant B.B. Midha, Company Officer
13. Lieutenant K.S. Yadav, Intelligence Officer
14. 2nd Lieutenant S.M. Karmarkar, Company Officer
15. 2nd Lieutenant N.N. Madappa, Company Officer
16. 2nd Lieutenant T.G. Verghese, Company Officer
17. Captain H.P. Sutradhar, Regimental Medical (Army Medical Corps), Officer

Honours and Awards

Vir Chakra:	Major I.P. Kharbanda Major Chandra Kant
Sena Medal:	Major S.P. Marwah Lance Naik Ram Naresh Singh
Mention-in-Despatches:	Lieutenant Colonel Himmeth Singh Major V.K. Dewan Major Shamsher Mehta (63 Cavalry)
Battalion Awards:	Battle Honour of Akhaura Theatre Honour of East Pakistan